first time
CROCHET

Inspiring | Educating | Creating | Entertaining

Brimming with creative inspiration, how-to projects, and useful information to enrich your everyday life, Quarto Knows is a favorite destination for those pursuing their interests and passions. Visit our site and dig deeper with our books into your area of interest: Quarto Creates, Quarto Cooks, Quarto Homes, Quarto Lives, Quarto Drives, Quarto Explores, Quarto Gifts, or Quarto Kids.

ISBN: 978-1-58923-825-1

Digital edition published in 2014
eISBN: 978-1-62788-368-9

10 9 8

Library of Congress Cataloging-in-Publication Data Available

Technical Editor: Karen J. Hay
Stitch Illustrations: Karen Manthey
Cover Design, Book Design, and Page Layout: Megan Jones Design
Step-out Photographs: Eleanor Dotson Carlisle
Cover Photo: Getty Images

Printed in China

first time
CROCHET
THE ABSOLUTE BEGINNER'S GUIDE

by Deborah Burger

Creative Publishing
international

contents

INTRODUCTION 7

CROCHET BASICS 9

GETTING STARTED 10
STARTING TO STITCH 20
CHAIN GANG BOA 27
SINGLE CROCHET IN ROWS 33
BRIGHT AND BOLD COASTERS 39
SINGLE CROCHET IN ROUNDS 44
ROLL BRIM CLOCHE 51
PHONE CARRIER 55
THE DOUBLE CROCHET STITCH 60
LONGITUDE SCARF 67
DOUBLE CROCHET MOTIFS IN LIVING COLOR 70
GRAB-AND-GO GRANNY BAG 77

PUTTING IT TOGETHER 83

COMBINING STITCHES, READING CHARTS 84
FLOWER POWER RETRO BEANIE 89
PATTERN STITCHES 94
COZY COWL AND CUFFS SET 103
MULTI-ROW STITCH PATTERNS—LOVELY LACE! 107
WINDFLOWER SHAWLETTE 113
A NEW STITCH 118
ANY FOOT SOFTY SLIPPERS 123
ABBREVIATIONS 126

ABOUT THE AUTHOR 127
INDEX 127

introduction

WELCOME TO THE VERSATILE, CREATIVE WORLD OF CROCHET! *FIRST TIME CROCHET* IS DESIGNED TO HELP YOU LEARN PAINLESSLY, BUILDING EACH NEW SKILL ON THE SUCCESS OF THOSE YOU'VE MASTERED. EASY-TO-FOLLOW INSTRUCTIONS WITH LOTS OF COLORFUL PHOTOGRAPHS HELP YOU GAIN CROCHET SKILLS STEP-BY-STEP.

A versatile fiber art, crochet can create softly draping fabric for shawls and sweaters, firm 3-dimensional stuffed toys and sculptures, sturdy or delicate fabrics according to need. The universal stitch symbols you'll learn in this book mean that patterns are shared across usual boundaries of language and culture, opening wide the doors to creative expression.

Each chapter of *First Time Crochet* introduces a new stitch or technique. You'll practice that skill, and then use it in making a beautiful project. For each lesson and project, the skills to be used or learned and the materials needed are listed for easy access. Troubleshooting boxes will help you evaluate the quality, possible mistakes, and means of correcting them, in your work as you progress. Tell Me More and Crochet Language boxes explain terms and processes without requiring you to turn to another page. Tips offer the sort of specific encouragement that builds confidence and ensures mastery. Each project lists the yarn required in generic terms of weight and fiber content, so you are free to choose from many suitable options. Projects can be made in the colors shown, or in your own favorites.

The first section, "Crochet Basics," acquaints you with the tools, materials, and methods for making basic crochet stitches in rows and in the round. The second section, "Putting It All Together," moves beyond the basics into the realm of textured and shaped fabric, pattern-stitches, and more complex sets of directions. After working through the book, you'll be able to read and follow standard patterns and diagrams, or crochet creatively from your own ideas.

Start each chapter by reading through the Skills and Materials boxes. Make sure the tools and materials for the lesson are at hand, so your learning and practice are not interrupted. Follow the written instructions and photographs, and don't skip the Practice Swatches. Practice pieces add to your understanding of the skill, and train your hands in their new task, so it's a very good habit to start. Use the Troubleshooting boxes and Tips to evaluate and improve your stitching, and then you'll be ready for the chapter's project.

Most of all, relax and enjoy your own blossoming creativity as you learn to crochet.

CROCHET BASICS

There's no better place to start than at the very beginning. To give you a firm foundation for learning to crochet, this section starts with essential facts about hooks and yarns. Next, you'll learn the basic stitches and the written language of crochet patterns. If crochet is completely new to you, you'll appreciate the detailed information and photos. Even if you have some crochet experience, you'll probably learn something new.

It's important to remember that you're training the muscles of your hands and fingers in movements new to them. Mistakes are a normal and natural part of the process. Holding and moving the hook and yarn will seem awkward at first; that's also part of the process. Relax! Stretch your shoulders and hands often; don't forget to breathe. Speed is not a measure of success, so feel free to stitch slowly, to take frequent breaks, and to enjoy the feeling of yarn passing through your fingers. Let's explore the basics of crochet!

getting started

THE TOOLS

At its simplest, crochet can be done with no tools at all, using the fingers to pull loops of yarn through other loops. But over the years, crocheters have found that a specialized hook eases the work and makes it possible to create much more complex and beautiful stitches. Generally, the only current uses for "finger crochet" are keeping lengths of electrical cord from tangling and keeping children occupied when they must sit still. All "real" crochet involves a hook of one sort or another, so let's take a look at the crochet hook.

The Crochet Hook

Hooks come in several different sizes and shapes, depending on their intended uses. But they all have the same parts, labeled in the photo below.

The tip of the hook is the part that's inserted between strands of yarn, and tips vary in shape from blunt to more pointed. The throat (or shank) and chin of the hook are the parts that do the actual work, catching a loop of yarn and pulling it through other loops. The shaft is what gives the hook its official size, and the size of the shaft

determines the size of the loops made. Some hooks have a thumb rest and some don't. When present, the thumb rest can make it easier to hold the hook, and also to loosen loops that have become too tight. On some brands of hooks, the thumb rest has been expanded into an ergonomic handle—crocheters with arthritis, carpal tunnel syndrome, and other hand health issues find that these handles help to keep their crochet hobby possible and pain-free. Some hooks, especially those made of wood, have decorative turning or carving at the end of the shaft. This shaping can help to provide balance, but is mostly an aesthetic element.

There are two basic shapes for hooks, and most crocheters find that they prefer one or the other. It's a good idea to try some crochet with each shape in the first few projects to discover which shape is the best for your own hands. Many crocheters find it extremely frustrating and difficult to work with the "wrong" hook shape, and only experimentation can determine the "right" hook for any particular crocheter. The

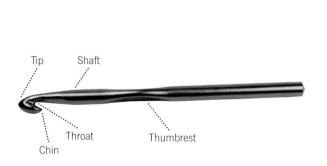

Tip Shaft

Throat

Chin Thumbrest

Boye/tapered hook

Bates/inline hook

major difference between the two kinds of hooks is in the shape of the throat.

An "inline" hook, also called a "Bates-shape" hook, has a throat as wide as the shaft, and the chin is formed by a straight cut into the hook's throat. Inline hooks usually have relatively blunt tips. The second major hook shape is the tapered or "Boye-shape" hook. Its throat becomes narrower from side to side as it approaches the tip, and the cut under the chin is also tapered. Tapered hooks usually have a relatively more pointed head. These names for the major hook shapes reference the two major companies that have provided crochet hooks for the last century, but many other companies and individuals now also create crochet hooks, using these standard shapes.

The hooks shown in use throughout this book are tapered, but that by no means implies superiority—it's simply the shape that works best for the author.

Hooks are available in a wide variety of materials as well as a wide variety of sizes. Tiny steel hooks are generally used for crocheting lace from cotton or silk thread. Steel hooks have their own sizing/naming system, different from the system used for all other hooks. Sizes start with 00, the largest, and progress through 14, with higher numbers denoting smaller hooks. This is similar to the system of "gauge" for steel wire.

The other most common materials for hooks are aluminum, wood, and bamboo. These larger hooks are usually used for crochet with yarn and other fibers. These hooks are commonly sized in the United States by a letter system. The system is gradually being replaced by simple measurements in millimeters. Many hooks are labeled with both a letter and a measurement, but letters alone are also still quite common. Generally .25 mm or .50 mm is the difference between two sizes, and the sizes with assigned letters are the easiest to find in craft stores.

Some older hooks and some custom made hooks are not labeled with their sizes, and sometimes the labels wear off with time and use. An inexpensive gauge tool, which will be discussed later, solves the "mystery hook" problem.

TIP *While working through the first few chapters, try out both shapes of hook, and then decide which works best for you!*

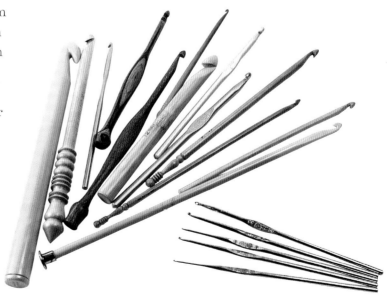

STEEL HOOK SIZES	ALUMINUM CROCHET HOOK SIZES
00 = 2.70 mm	
0 = 2.55 mm	B/1 = 2.25 mm
1 = 2.35 mm	C/2 = 2.75 mm
2 = 2.20 mm	D/3 = 3.25 mm
3 = 2.10 mm	E/4 = 3.5 mm
4 = 1.75 mm	F/5 = 3.75 mm
5 = 1.70 mm	G/6 = 4 mm
6 = 1.60 mm	7 = 4.5 mm
7 = 1.50 mm	H/8 = 5 mm
8 = 1.40 mm	I/9 = 5.5 mm
9 = 1.25 mm	J/10 = 6 mm
10 = 1.15 mm	K/10½ = 6.5 mm
11 = 1.05 mm	L/11 = 8 mm
12 = 1.00 mm	M/N/13 = 9 mm
13 = 0.95 mm	N/P/15 = 10 mm
14 = 0.90 mm	P/Q = 15 mm
	Q = 16 mm
	S = 19 mm

FIBERS FOR CROCHET

Crochet consists of looped fiber. We've discussed the hook that creates the loop, but it's also important to understand some of the variety of materials that wrap around the hooks! Besides the traditional white cotton or silk thread, crocheters commonly use yarn made of various fibers, which is available in a variety of sizes. The size or thickness of the yarn is as important as the size of the hook, to determine the softness or firmness, drape or stiffness, of the fabric created; each type and size of yarn has appropriate uses. The packaging of yarn or thread usually gives information about the thickness, fiber content and its care, and length in yards or meters, of the hank or ball. We'll examine those labels closely later, but let's look at the types of fiber first.

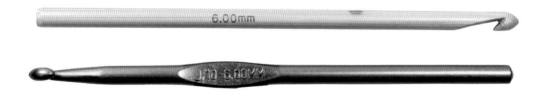

Sizes are commonly labeled on thumbrest or shaft.

Thread

Many of the traditional uses of crochet involved making lace from thread. Most thread made for crochet is cotton. It's available in both "mercerized" and unmercerized states. Thread consists of very tightly spun fibers, and has no ability to stretch when pulled. Any stretch in the fabric is produced by the particular stitches used, and still has very little "memory" or ability to bounce back to its original shape after being stretched. Mercerization reduces the cotton's ability to absorb moisture, but adds beauty to the finished object. A tablecloth, for instance, might be made of mercerized cotton to reduce absorption of stains and spills and provide a polished appearance. On the other hand, unmercerized thread creates lace for garments that is less stiff and scratchy feeling, because it has less polish on its surface. Thread is available in numbered sizes, and like the steel hooks, the higher numbers denote finer threads. "Bedspread Cotton" or #10 thread is the most common size. #5 cotton thread is commonly used for summer garments and accessories, as is #3, "Perle Cotton." Embroidery floss is another form of cotton thread sometimes used for crochet. Its brilliant colors can provide wonderful accents in white or ecru lace. Perle Cotton and embroidery floss are usually sold in twisted or folded hanks, which must be wound into balls before use for crochet, or terrible tangling will result. Thread in size 5 and 10 are usually wound on a cardboard spool or cone, ready for immediate use.

Left to right: #30, #10, #5, and Perle threads

Yarn

The word "yarn" refers to fibers spun much more loosely than thread. Yarn, even when actually thinner than thread, is distinct because the looser spin allows it to stretch. Crocheting with yarn requires less tension in the hands, and provides a wide variety of finished effects. Regardless of the fiber content, yarn is categorized by size. The Craft Yarn Council of America has developed a set of standard size ranges, and project patterns refer to these names and numbers.

STANDARD YARN WEIGHT SYSTEM

Categories of yarn, gauge ranges, and recommended needle and hook sizes

Yarn Weight Symbol & Category Names	0	1	2	3	4	5	6
Type of Yarns in Category	Fingering 10-count crochet thread	Sock, Fingering, Baby	Sport, Baby	DK, Light Worsted	Worsted, Afghan, Aran	Chunky, Craft, Rug	Bulky, Roving
Crochet Gauge* Ranges in Single Crochet to 4 inch	32–42 double crochets**	21–32 sts	16–20 sts	12–17 sts	11–14 sts	8–11 sts	5–9 sts
Recommended Hook in Metric Size Range	Steel*** 1.6–1.4 mm	2.25—3.5 mm	3.5—.5 mm	4.5—5.5 mm	5.5—6.5 mm	6.5—9 mm	9 mm and larger
Recommended Hook U.S. Size Range	Steel*** 6, 7, 8 Regular hook B–1	B–1 to E–4	E–4 to 7	7 to I–9	I–9 to K–10½	K–10½ to M–13	M–13 and larger

* GUIDELINES ONLY: The above reflect the most commonly used gauges and needle or hook sizes for specific yarn categories.

** Lace weight yarns are usually knitted or crocheted on larger needles and hooks to create lacy, openwork patterns. Accordingly, a gauge range is difficult to determine. Always follow the gauge stated in your pattern.

*** Steel crochet hooks are sized differently from regular hooks—the higher the number, the smaller the hook, which is the reverse of regular hook sizing.

Craft Yarn Council of America

You'll notice that each of the categories is actually a range of sizes, and while all yarns labeled with that number fall within its range, there can still be some variety between the size of different yarns within the same category! The system is a guide when choosing yarns, but it's important to remember that not all yarns in one category will necessarily make good substitutes for one another.

Besides size differences, yarn is made from many different materials. Cotton yarn is similar in some ways to cotton thread, except that it's spun more loosely. Worsted (#4) cotton yarn is often called "kitchen cotton" and is used for making highly absorbent and often beautiful dishcloths and towels. However, cotton yarn can also be used to make sweaters, scarves, and other accessories, especially when blended with other fibers. Cotton's ability to absorb moisture makes it a great choice for summer garments. Wool is spun from sheep's' fleece, and has several wonderful properties. It is the only fiber that can help retain body heat even when wet. Wool also repels water, and has great stretch memory. Other animals' hair is also commonly spun into yarn, as well: alpaca is the warmest fiber, but has a very delicate structure; mohair is sturdy and can add a fuzzy or "haloed" texture to yarn, and to the fabric made from it; llamas, yaks, camels, and angora rabbits also provide very soft hair for yarn.

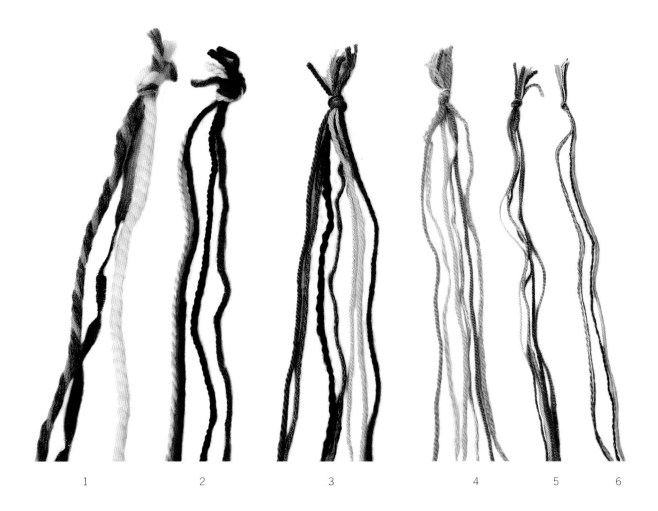

1   2   3   4   5   6

Yarn purchased in a loose hank or skein must be wound into a ball or cake before beginning to crochet. You may wonder why many of the finer yarns are sold in this format, requiring an extra step of preparation! Commercially wound yarns often contain serious tangles at their centers. While it's inconvenient to have to untangle the yarn, sturdy yarns made of mostly synthetic fibers are not harmed by the process. On the other hand, delicate fibers, such as silk or alpaca; or yarn that has been spun with haloed or bouclé texture can be seriously damaged by the untangling process. In addition, sitting for months on a shelf can stretch natural fibers, reducing the beauty and function of the yarn when it's used. To avoid these problems, many natural fiber yarns, fine and textured yarns, and other higher quality yarns are sold in loosely wound hanks or skeins.

Yarn purchased for future use should be stored in skein form, to avoid stretching out the fibers by winding and leaving the wound balls to sit for more than a few weeks. When ready to use yarn purchased in skein form, there are two methods commonly used for winding: by hand or with a pair of tools called a swift and a ball winder.

tell me more
HANK AND SKEIN are interchangeable words that refer to loosely wound lengths of yarn, whether twisted for safety, or hanging loosely in a large single loop. "Pull skeins" have already been wound by the manufacturer so that the yarn is ready to use, either from the center or the outside.

Winding by Hand

1   To wind by hand, remove the label from the skein of yarn and open the large loop, carefully removing any threads used to keep the skein's strands untangled. Locate one end of the yarn, and let it hang free.

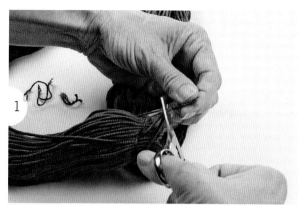

2   Drape the skein of yarn over the back of a chair, or the hands of a partner. Ideally, the distance should be wide enough to keep the strands of yarn snug—neither stretched tightly nor sagging loosely.

3   Unwind a yard or so of the yarn, and wind it around three fingers, about 20 times around.

4   Remove the yarn from fingers, and fold the grouped loops in half. Now continue to wrap, but across the grain, perpendicular to the direction of the first set of wraps.

As the ball grows, turn from time to time, to wrap in another direction. Continue until the entire skein is wound into a ball. The ball will be used from the outside. To avoid its natural tendency to roll around, place the ball in a bowl when crocheting with it.

YARN VOCABULARY

Smooth or plain—just as it sounds, no real discernable texture to the yarn. Plain textured yarns are the easiest to crochet with, and allow special textures in the actual stitches to show to best advantage.

Loft—the ability of a yarn to be squeezed smaller (feel "squishy"), and to naturally expand to fill space. Loft is created by air space between the fibers in the yarn.

Twist—the tightness and direction that the fibers are spun together to create the yarn.

Ply—smaller strands of spun fiber that are twisted together to create yarn. A "single" is not plied; its fibers are spun in only one direction. When singles are twisted together, they form a yarn less likely to kink and knot in use. "Worsted" yarn is often made of 4 plies; DK or "Sport" of 3.

Halo—any visible fibers sticking out from the main, twisted core of the yarn. These create a fuzzy texture in the yarn, and in fabric made from the yarn.

Thick and thin—just as it sounds. Some yarns are intentionally varying in their diameter. These yarns are then sized by averaging the thickest parts and thinnest parts, to fit in the CYCA sizing system.

Slubs—as the word sounds, slubs are intentional blobs of unspun or knotted fiber, included in the yarn to add textural interest.

Bouclé—refers to loops in yarn, created by twisting two plies together at different rates of speed. The loops can be large or small, and create a haloed effect, as the loops spread out from the yarn's core.

Bloom—refers to a yarn's ability to expand or develop a halo after the fabric is made. Yarns that bloom may start out with a smooth or plain texture, but later develop a fuzzy surface. This characteristic can make it easier to create fuzzy surfaces, since the yarn "works" like a plain yarn, and develops its softer surface later. However, yarns that bloom are not a good choice for showing off textured stitching.

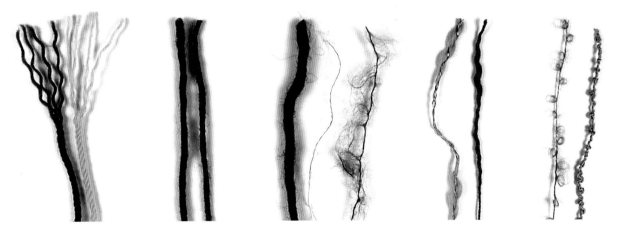

From left to right: smooth or plain with several plies, smooth single, yarns with halo, plied thick and thin with slubs, boucle yarn

NOTIONS

Besides a hook and yarn, there are many notions to choose from. Only a few of them are essential, though! The necessary notions are:

Scissors—a small, pointed pair of sharp scissors will make it easy to be accurate in cutting yarn exactly where it needs to be cut.

Large-eyed yarn needle—used for weaving tails of yarn into the completed fabric, and for sewing together pieces of a project. Needles are available in either plastic or steel, but steel tends to glide through the fabric more easily, enhancing the accuracy and invisibility of seams.

Clear ruler—essential for measuring "gauge" or the size of the actual stitches. Correct fit of garments depends on knowing the number of stitches per inch (cm) in a particular project. A six-inch ruler is long enough for this purpose. Using a clear, as opposed to a solid ruler, makes it easy to see and count the stitches being measured.

Tape measure—36" (1 m) will be sufficient for most purposes, but many crocheters use a 60" (2 m) measure for larger projects, such as afghans.

Stitch markers—anything from scraps of contrasting yarn, to safety pins, bobby pins, paper clips, commercially or custom made markers, that can be placed into a particular stitch and later removed. Avoid the solid ring markers used in knitting, as they cannot be removed from crochet without wire cutters!

Sticky notes—used for keeping track of the current row in a written pattern.

Hook gauge—this little tool identifies the exact size of hooks without labels, and hooks that have been inaccurately labeled by the manufacturer. Inline hooks can be measured with a knitting needle gauge, but tapered hooks are best measured with a V-gauge, as shown in the picture (green plastic square with cut notches). To measure a hook, place the round shaft of the hook, between throat and thumbrest, in the smallest space it will fully fill in the gauge. Read the measurement in millimeters or letter size for that space.

Keep all the necessary notions in a zippered plastic bag or any other convenient container, as they will be used often in most projects. Many commercial notions bags are available, but any appropriately sized, easy-to-open container will do just fine!

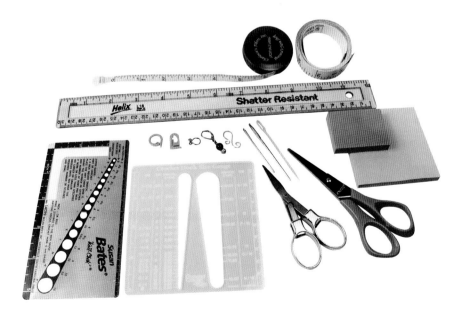

starting to stitch

HOW TO HOLD THE CROCHET HOOK

There is no one "right way" to hold the crochet hook, but some are more effective, efficient, and healthier for the hand and wrist than others. The three most common hook holds are the Pencil Hold, the Knife Hold, and the Chopstick Hold. The Pencil Hold was developed at a time when ladies wanted to appear graceful and elegant while engaged in any activity, and its primary feature is that the "pinkie" finger can easily be held at an elegant angle. However, this under-hand hold requires much more movement of the wrist in every stitch, which can lead to repetitive stress injuries, such as carpal tunnel syndrome. The Chopstick Hold is similar, in that it requires constant bend in the wrist, and also places the least coordinated fingers in position to control loops of yarn on the hook. However, many cro-cheters continue to find one of these to be their preferred hold, and can be successful by taking extra breaks to rest the wrist, and/or wearing a supportive fingerless glove. The Knife Hold was developed more recently, in order to pro-vide increased control of loops on the hook and increased comfort for the hand and wrist. This overhand method has gained popularity as the crafting population has grown more concerned with fun and health than with elegance. Try the different holds in the first two projects, to find the best style for your hands.

Most people will hold the hook in the right hand, and the yarn in the left hand. Because crochet uses both hands, even left-handed cro-cheters are not disadvantaged, and often find it a distinct advantage to hold and move the yarn, instead of the hook, with their dominant hand.

Pencil Hold—hook over top of hand, between thumb and first finger

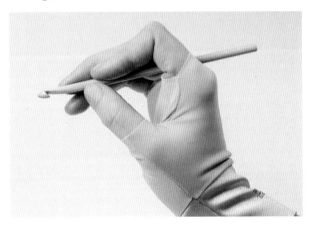

Chopstick Hold—hook over top of hand, between fingers

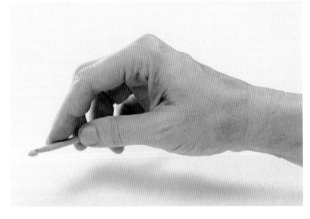

Knife or Overhand Hold—hand over top of hook, wrist in neutral position

However, some "lefties" do prefer to hold the hook in the left hand, and reverse for themselves all directional instructions. The photographs in this book all show the hook in the right hand, even though the pictured crocheter writes with her left! Whether to move the yarn more, or the hook more, is a personal decision, but in either case, there is an initial period of feeling awkward, regardless of hand preference!

HOW TO HOLD THE YARN

There is also no one "right" way to hold the yarn, and each crocheter goes through a process of experimentation to find a satisfactory balance between firm control and necessary flow as the yarn is used in each stitch. The photos here show three common, effective methods. Notice that in each, the index finger is extended, ready to move the yarn where needed, and that other fingers regulate the tension or flow of the yarn as it is used.

Don't be afraid to experiment, and don't expect to settle a yarn hold in the first few projects! It takes time and repetition for fingers and yarn to become accustomed to working together.

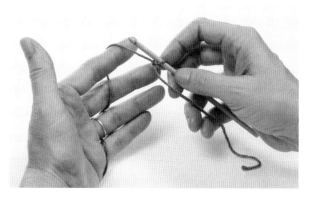

"Woven" yarn hold: Yarn from the working ball simply passes over and under alternate fingers. Tension is increased by squeezing fingers together when needed.

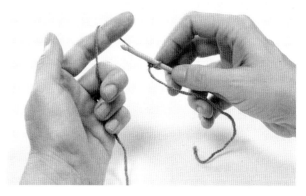

Simple "fist" hold: Yarn from the working ball is held in the fist. Tension is increased by closing the fist.

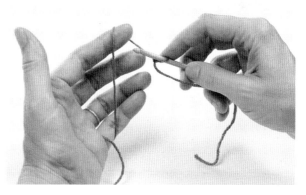

Looped tension hold: Yarn passes between pinkie and ring fingers, around pinkie and across palm, then around index finger. Tension is increased by curling the pinkie finger and holding it against ring finger.

HOW TO GET YARN ON THE HOOK—THE SLIP KNOT

All crochet begins with a slip knot. This simple knot is identical to one half of a "bow" when tying shoes. Start by making a loop, about 8" (20.5 cm) from the end of the yarn, with the yarn tail away from you, behind the circle that's been formed. Push the tail through to form a loop; tighten the loop by pulling the yarn attached to the main ball.

Place the slip knot on the hook, with the working yarn away from you.

When a slip knot is formed correctly, pulling on the tail will tighten the loop, and pulling on the working yarn will tighten the knot. Pull the tail to snug the loop to the shaft of the hook. It needs to be close enough that "daylight" doesn't show through, but loose enough to move easily up and down the shaft of the hook. Use the index finger to hold that loop in place and prevent it from spinning around the hook. It may also be helpful to spend a few minutes practicing using the index finger to move the loop slightly up and down the shaft of the hook without losing control of it. Everything is now in place to make the first crochet stitch!

CROCHET LANGUAGE

Working yarn—the yarn attached to the ball of yarn from which you are working. In crochet, the working yarn is always held at the back of the fabric being created.

Tail—the short length of yarn extending from the slip knot.

Front of the work—the side closest to you as you crochet.

Back of the work—the side of the work facing away from the crocheter.

Right side—the side of the fabric that will be most viewed when the project is complete. When working back and forth in rows, the right side and wrong side will alternately be facing you, and when facing you, will be called the front of the work.

Wrong side—the side of the fabric that will be less viewed (i.e., inside of a garment) when project is complete.

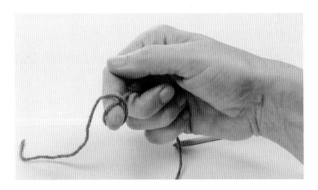

Yarn loop with tail behind.

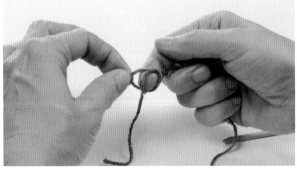

Pushing tail through to form loop.

THE CHAIN STITCH

MATERIALS

○ Worsted (#4) yarn

○ Crochet hook size H, I, or J (5.00, 5.5 or 6.00 mm)

1 With the chin of the hook facing you, and the right index finger holding the loop on the hook, the left hand brings the yarn over the top of the hook, from the back, and down across the throat of the hook. The left thumb and second finger pull down on the slip knot to open up a small space at the bottom of the loop on the hook, while the left index finger moves the working yarn.

2 The right hand turns the hook downward to a "6 o'clock" position, catching the wrapped yarn with the hook, and pulls it through the loop already on the hook. The finger holding the loop on the hook lets go at this point, and will take its place to control the new loop, now on the hook. Do Not pull or tighten the stitch once completed. The chain now being formed serves as a base for the next row of stitches, and must be made loosely. To work the following row, the hook will be inserted between the threads of each chain stitch, so be sure to work loosely enough to allow insertion.

Correct direction for yarn over—hook is under yarn as yarn comes over the hook from the back, and down across the hook at the front.

Wrong direction for yarnover. If yarn is wrapped in this direction, the stitches will twist, affecting the appearance and function of the fabric.

Hook pulling yarn through loop.

Completed first chain stitch.

Practice making chains until it becomes a fluid motion and the resulting loops become even in their size and shape.

Pattern instructions will nearly always start with "Chain ____," with a number filling in the blank. To count chains, lay the work flat, so that the side with a flat braided or sideways Vs appearance is facing up. Each V is one stitch. All other crochet stitches will also have the sideways V at the top of every stitch, and this is what is counted to determine the number of completed stitches. Never count the loop currently on the hook—there was a loop on the hook before a stitch was made, and as it's replaced continually by a new loop, it is still not actually part of any stitch. Start counting with the last V in line before the tight knot at the end, and stop at the V immediately below the hook.

CROCHET LANGUAGE

Yarn over: abbreviated "yo" in patterns, always refers to wrapping the yarn from back to front over the top of the hook and down across the throat of the hook.

Chain stitch is described as "yarn over hook, pull through one loop" and is abbreviated in patterns as "ch: yo and pull through 1." Patterns do not generally describe this step, but assume that the crocheter knows how to make a chain, and simply state the number of chain stitches (ch) to make.

1   2   3   4   5   6   7   8   9   10

practice swatch

MATERIALS

- Worsted (#4) yarn
- J (6 mm) or K (6.50–7 mm) hook

SKILLS

- Fluency with the chain stitch
- How to fasten off finished work

TROUBLESHOOTING

If the chain spirals or twists slightly as it grows longer, the stitches are a little too tight. "Kinking" or "elbows" in the length of chain indicate that some of the stitches are looser and others tighter than their neighbors. It's better to work toward making them all a bit looser. A tight chain may appear tidy or elegant, but will cause frustration and difficulty later, when the hook must be inserted into those stitches.

Make a slip knot and start chaining. Each time the loop is pulled through, a stitch is completed, and the next chain stitch starts. Gradually, try to make the chains of even size and large enough that the hook tip can easily be inserted into each chain.

When each length of chain is as long as you like, "fasten off the work" thus: cut the working yarn about 8" (20.5 cm) away from the work. Use the hook to pull this tail of yarn right through the last chain stitch made. The last stitch is now locked and will not unravel. This is the way all crochet ends.

TIP *You can pull yarn from the outside or the inside of a ball, though pulling from the inside is a simpler motion and doesn't cause the yarn ball to roll around as much. In either case, even tension is easier to achieve by pulling out a yard or two at a time instead of requiring the action of the hook to pull yarn from the skein for each stitch.*

Left to right: ideal tension, tension too tight, uneven tension

CHAIN GANG BOA

Here's a fashion statement crocheted entirely in chain stitch! Whether you make the plain or beaded version, this fun and quick scarf will be a great addition to any accessory wardrobe.

MATERIALS

YARN

- Less than 1 skein each (25 yds [23 m]) or so) of 5 to 7 different yarns, a mix of light worsted (#3), worsted (#4), and chunky (#5) in your choice of fiber. Plain textured yarns will be better than slubby or haloed yarns. Choose colors that coordinate and please you

HOOKS

- H, I, and J (5.00, 5.50, and 6.00 mm)

NOTIONS

- Scissors
- Large-eyed yarn or darning needle
- Measuring tape or yard stick

FINISHED SIZE

- Approximately 65" long × 3" wide (165 × 7.5 cm)

GAUGE

- With H hook and light worsted yarn, 100 ch = 22" to 26" (56 to 66 cm). Exact gauge is not important for this project.

STITCHES AND ABBREVIATIONS USED

- chain = ch
- stitch(es) = st(s)
- approximately = approx
- yard(s) = yd(s)

SKILLS

- Fluency with the slip knot and chain stitch in different combinations of hook and yarn
- How to weave in yarn ends securely at the finishing stage of a project

INSTRUCTIONS

1 Arrange the yarns in three groups, according to visible thickness. The H (5.00 mm) hook will be used with the thinnest group, the I (5.50 mm) hook with the mid-sized group, and the J (6.00 mm) hook with the thickest yarns.

2 Leaving a 6" to 8" (15 50 20.5 cm) tail, make a slip knot in one of the thin (Group A) yarns. Place the loop on the H (5.00 mm) hook and snug it to a natural fit.

3 Make 100 chain stitches, trying for a loose, even size to the loops. Don't worry if the chain seems to twist; it's normal and only means the work is a little on the tight side. Work toward even tension or gauge. Measure the length of the chain, laid flat but not stretched. Don't count the beginning tail in your measurement, only the chain itself. Somewhere between 22" to 26" (56 to 66 cm) indicates the correct size of each stitch.

4 Continue to chain until the chain is approximately 72" (1.85 m) long. (About 280-300 stitches, but this is a general guideline; accurate counting is not necessary.)

5 Fasten off: cut the yarn, leaving a 6" to 8" (15 to 20.5 cm) tail, and pull the tail through the last chain loop made.

6 Repeat steps 2 to 5 with the H (5.00 mm) hook and the other Group A yarns, until there are 2 to 4 separate pieces of chain, each measuring about 72" (1.85 m) long.

7 With the I (5.50 mm) hook and yarns from the midsized group, Group B, repeat steps 2 to 5. Because the hook and yarn are larger, the gauge will be different for this group. The 100 chains should measure between 30" to 33" (76 to 84 cm). About 225 to 235 total chain stitches will make the 72"

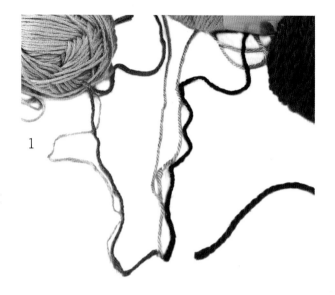

1

(1.85 m) length. Repeat with the yarns from Group B, until you have 2 to 4 Group B lengths of chain.

8 Using the J (6.00 mm) hook and the thickest group (Group C) of yarns, repeat steps 2 to 5. Gauge with this hook and yarn combination will yield a gauge measurement of about 100 stitches = 32" to 34" (81.5 to 86.5 cm). The 72" (1.85 m) length of completed chain stitches will consist of about 210 to 220 stitches. Repeat this step at least once, so there are two or more chains made with Group C yarns.

TIP *If, in spite of careful math and measurement, one or more of the chains turns out more than a couple of inches longer than the rest, it's easy to adjust the length at this point. Gently pull the fastened yarn tail back through the last stitch, and pull out the last few stitches made, till the piece is approximately as long as all the others. Then pull the tail through the last chain loop. A slight variation (1" to 2" [2.5 to 5 cm]) in the lengths of chain will enhance the final project, but one significantly longer chain will detract.*

9 There are now seven to eleven lengths of chain, in various thicknesses, each about 72" (1.85 m) long. Weave in both tails of each chain, as follows: Thread one tail onto the darning needle; sew in and out of chain loops, working up the chain, for about 2" (5 cm).

(continued)

10 Reverse direction and sew in and out, being careful not to "un-do" the first line of stitches, working back toward the end of the chain. Cut the tail with scissors, close to the end of the chain, and give a slight tug to tighten the remaining bit of tail. The tug will pull the last bit of tail inside the end of the chain. Repeat for opposite end of chain, and for each end of all chains.

11 Tie a simple overhand knot in each end of each chain length, as close to the end as possible, and tug it tight. The resulting chains will all be of slightly different lengths.

12 Fold each chain length in half and mark the center. (This is easily done by tying all the chains together temporarily, at their centers, with a contrasting piece of yarn.)

13 With the centers of all chains together, tie an overhand knot (one loop and pull the end through) near each end, so that 3" to 6" (7.5 to 15 cm) of all the chains remain beyond the knot. All chains are now joined together at each end.

14 Tie another knot half-way between each end-knot and the marked center. Remove center marker.

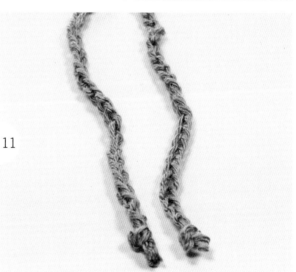

CROCHET LANGUAGE

Most crochet patterns are written in a short-hand of standard abbreviations. A list of all these common abbreviations appears on page 126. Here is what a standard pattern for the Chain Gang Boa would look like:

INSTRUCTIONS

1 With H (5.00mm) hook and each Group A yarn, ch approx. 72" (185 cm) (about 280-300 sts). Fasten off. Make a total of 2-4 Group A pieces.

2 Repeat 3–5 times with I (5.50mm) hook and Group B yarns. Repeat 2-4 times with J hook and Group C yarns.

ASSEMBLY/FINISHING

Weave in tails on all chains. Tie a knot at each end of each finished chain. Mark centers of chains. With centers held together, tie a knot 3-6" (7.5 to 15 cm) from each end, bundling all chains together. Tie another knot half-way from each end knot to center. Remove center marker.

VARIATION

Try variations on the Chain Gang! Use different combinations of yarn, and different numbers of chains. Add a bead or button to each end of each chain just before weaving in the tail. (Be sure to purchase beads with a large enough center hole to accommodate yarn needle and yarn.)

single crochet in rows

One of the wonderful aspects of crochet is the number of options—such as those for holding the hook and yarn. Options exist, too, as we begin to work stitches into the chain and build a fabric. Beginners can find the number of choices a bit overwhelming! Knowing what factors or circumstances make one choice preferable to another can help to dispel the fear of "doing it wrong."

This chapter introduces the single crochet stitch (abbreviated "sc") and shows various options for working single crochet into the chain. Then rows of single crochet stitches are worked on top of one another to create a useful fabric. The practice swatch will help to address common errors and the project will use the new skills to make a set of thirsty, bright coasters.

THE SINGLE CROCHET STITCH

Start by making a slip knot and placing it on the size K (6.50 mm) hook. Chain 11 loosely. Remove the K hook from the work and insert the J (6.00 mm) hook. Even many experienced crocheters typically make the foundation chain with a hook larger than the one that will do the actual stitching. This practice is especially helpful if there's any doubt as to whether the chain stitches are loose enough to work in.

In naming the stitches to determine where to insert the hook, stitches are counted from the hook back toward the original slip knot. The loop on the hook is not counted, and the chain immediately below the hook is called the first chain. Single crochet rows always start with one unused chain. This "turning chain" provides space for maneuvering the hook as the row begins, and creates an even edge to the fabric being created.

MATERIALS

YARN
○ Worsted weight (#4) yarn

HOOKS
○ Sizes I (5.50 mm), J (6.00 mm), and K (6.50 mm)

NOTIONS
○ Scissors
○ Yarn needle
○ 2 stitch markers

SKILLS
○ Where to insert the hook in the chain to begin stitching
○ How to correctly form the single crochet stitch
○ How to end one row and begin the next

So to begin, locate the second chain from the hook by counting the sideways Vs on the front of the chain. This is the first space in which to work a single crochet stitch. Each chain consists of 3 strands: the lower or front arm of the V is called the Front Loop; the upper or back arm of the V is the Back Loop, and the central strand, best seen from the back of the chain, is the Bottom Bump or Back Bar. The first choice to make is exactly where to insert the hook. Successful fabric can be created by inserting the hook at any point in each chain! But there are some factors to keep in mind. It's easiest to insert the hook right into the middle of the chain, under the Back Loop and over the other two threads. This method starts the project quickly and easily, but stretches each chain stitch out, leaving a hole and sometimes making it difficult to see the next chain in line. This also creates a fabric edge without "finished" appearance, and the item will need an edging. Inserting the hook only under the lower edge, under the Front Loop, has the same effect. If an edging will later be worked or if the pattern directs that later work will also be started in the opposite side of the chain, then this method is entirely appropriate; although it may take a bit of practice to be confident in finding the next adjacent chain.

Inserting the hook under two of the strands, whether under the Front and Back Loops, or under the Back Loop and Bottom Bump, will not stretch out the stitch. However, the resulting edge will probably need an edging in order to appear the same as the opposite end of the piece of fabric.

The third option is to turn the chain over and insert the hook under the Bottom Bump. This method is a little trickier at the start, but creates a completely finished edge, identical to the one that will exist at the other end of the work, where the tops of stitches form the edge.

Back Loop only.

Front Loop only.

Front and Back Loops.

Back Loop and Bottom Bump.

(continued)   *Bottom Bump only.*

For this lesson, it's more important to consistently locate each chain and make just one stitch in it, than to insist on one particular insertion.

1 Insert the hook into the second stitch from the hook, by poking the tip in, from front to back, moving the tip of the hook away from you.

2 With the hook now at the back of the work, and the working yarn being held at the back by the left hand, the hook will be just beneath the working yarn. Catch the working yarn with the chin of the hook, and pull that new loop toward you through the work, to the front. This step is commonly abbreviated as "yo and draw up a loop." There are now two loops on the hook.

3 Yarn over just as in making chains, and pull the new loop through both of the loops on the hook. This step is abbreviated as "yo and pull through 2." One single crochet stitch is now complete. It consists of two vertical "feet" in the chain, and a new Front Loop and Back Loop at its top.

4 Locate the next chain, immediately to the left of the stitch just completed. Repeat steps 1 to 3 to form the next single crochet stitch.

5 Continue in this manner until each chain has one single crochet stitch in it. There should be 10 single crochets, and they are counted, same as chains, by looking at the braided top edge of the work. The tops of the stitches appear just like a row of chain—a series of sideways Vs. Count the stitches to make sure that there are 10.

Yarn over at back of work.

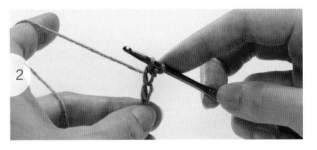

Loop drawn up, 2 loops on hook.

Hook pulling yo through 2 loops.

Completed single crochet stitch, arrow shows location of next chain stitch in line.

TROUBLESHOOTING

If there are fewer than 10 stitches it means that one or more chains were missed or skipped. These may appear as holes or spaces between the bases of the single crochet stitches.

On the other hand, if there are more than 10 stitches, it means that two or more stitches have been worked into the same chain. These can be located by finding single crochets crowded together, with their "feet" angled instead of straight. Also, the row will bend like an elbow wherever two or more stitches are worked in the same chain. (This characteristic will actually be very useful later in creating different shapes with crochet.)

If you have more or fewer than 10 stitches, use the troubleshooting photos to locate the problem. Remove the hook from the final loop and gently pull stitches out, just back to the spot where the problem occurred. Stick the hook back into the top of the last "good stitch," and begin working again.

Missed or skipped chains result in fewer stitches, spaces between stitches, and the work bends upward at the ends.

Working more than one single crochet (sc) in a chain (ch) results in more than 10 stitches in the row and causes the work to bend downward.

5

Completed first row of 10 single crochet (sc) stitches.

TIP *The most difficult row, for most crocheters, is the first one, working into the chain. There is little to hold on to, and the stitches are less visually obvious. Take your time with this step and remember to work loosely, so there is room to insert the hook into the tops of the stitches of Row 1 when you get to Row 2.*

Turning the Work

Before beginning Row 2, where single crochets will be worked in the tops of the stitches of Row 1, you must do two things: turn the work so that the unworked tops of Row 1 stretch out to the left, and chain one (the "turning chain"). Many beginners also find it useful to place a stitch marker in the top of the first stitch worked in each row.

Look at the row just completed and place a marker in the first stitch you made. The marker can be slipped onto the front or the back loop of the top of the stitch, at the opposite (beginning) end of the row from where the hook is now situated. Also mark the last stitch, the one most recently completed. The first stitch of the following row will be made in this marked stitch, then work in every stitch including the marked stitch at the other end of the row.

Marking helps to make sure every stitch in every row is worked. It doesn't matter which of these (the marking, the ch1, or the turning) is done first, though patterns may specify one way or another. Turn the work as if you were turning the page of a book, with the tops of Row 1's stitches still at the top of the work. Chain 1 (yo and pull through 1 loop), and Row 2 will begin.

Ready to start Row 2, blue marker is first stitch made in Row 1.

Row 2—Working sc into sc

As before, the loop on the hook will not count. The loop immediately below the hook is the turning chain. Locate the first actual stitch of the row, immediately below or to the left of the turning chain. Insert the hook under both the front and back loops. It is possible to work under only one of the loops, but that's a different stitch and creates a different texture to the fabric. The standard way to work all basic crochet stitches is to insert under both loops of the top V. When a pattern intends that only one loop is used, that will be clearly stated.

Complete one sc stitch in each stitch across the row. The three steps of each stitch are the same as for the first row, except that most people find it easier to work into sc stitches than into chains!

Correct hook insertion into a sc.

CROCHET LANGUAGE

In a standard pattern, directions for the two rows just completed, will read like this:

Foundation—ch 11.

Row 1: Sc in 2nd ch from hook and in each ch across. Turn.

Row 2: Ch 1, sc in each st across. Turn.

practice swatch

MATERIALS

YARN
- Worsted yarn
- J (6.00 mm) hook
- Yarn needle

GAUGE
- Exact gauge is not important for this project

STITCHES AND ABBREVIATIONS USED
- chain = ch
- single crochet = sc
- stitch(es) = st(s)

Using the same hook and yarn, follow this pattern, written in standard pattern language. If necessary, refer to previous "Tell Me More" explanations to help in understanding pattern language:

Foundation: Ch 13.

Row 1: Sc in 2nd ch from hook and in each ch across row. Turn.

Rows 2–8: Ch 1, sc in each st across. Turn. At end of Row 8, fasten off.

Finishing: Weave in tails. (This is the same process used to sew in the tails in the Chain Gang Boa project—simply thread the tail onto a yarn needle and run it through the inside of a row in one direction, then vertically through two or three rows, then opposite to the first direction in another row.)

TROUBLESHOOTING

It's normal for small swatches of single crochet to curl diagonally, from the lower right corner and the upper left corner. This is due to the shape of the stitch. Because curling is more pronounced if the work is a little tight, one way to minimize curling is to work loosely. Most projects will also call for an edging to be worked around the outside of single crocheted pieces, or for seams. Either of these finishing steps usually eliminates the curling. Blocking finished work is another way to flatten it, and will be discussed in detail in a later chapter.

Normal curling of edges.

BRIGHT AND BOLD COASTERS

These coasters can be made of either cotton or cotton/hemp blend. Acrylic yarn does not absorb liquid, so is less useful for coasters. The crochet will be worked at a tighter gauge, to provide a stiff, solid fabric, capable of protecting furniture. Each coaster is made from two layers of crochet fabric joined together with crocheted edging.

MATERIALS

For set of 4 coasters

YARN
- Light worsted (#4) cotton or cotton/hemp blend yarn, about 100 yds (92 m) each, in 3 colors

HOOK
- Size G (4.25 mm) or size needed to match gauge

NOTIONS
- Yarn needle
- Stitch markers (optional)

FINISHED SIZE
- Approximately 4½" wide by 4" tall (11.5 × 10 cm)

GAUGE
- 15 stitches = 3½" (9 cm), 14 rows = 3¼" (8.5 cm). Exact gauge is not necessary for this project

STITCHES AND ABBREVIATIONS USED
- chain = ch
- single crochet = sc
- slip stitch = sl st
- stitch(es) = st(s)

SKILLS
- How to read a pattern with several steps
- How to measure and adjust gauge
- How to attach a new yarn and work single crochet edging, including corner increases
- How to join two stitches with a slip stitch
- How to finish a project with steam blocking

tell me more

GAUGE is a measure of the size of each stitch. Patterns tell the size of the designer's stitches, and if a finished project is to be the stated size, your stitches must be the same size. Gauge is stated as the number of stitches equal to a number of inches (centimeters), and the number of rows equal to a number of inches (centimeters). Patterns usually state whether the gauge is essential or not for the success of the project.

INSTRUCTIONS

Note: Stitch counts are listed in {brackets} at the end of row instructions. For each coaster make one square with A and one with B.

Foundation: Ch 16.

Row 1: Sc in 2nd ch from hook and in each ch across. Turn. {15 sc}

Row 2: Ch 1, sc in each st across. Turn. {15 sc}

Rows 3–14: Repeat Row 2.

At end of Row 14, measure the row gauge. Flatten your piece and measure to see whether it's larger or smaller than the stated 3¼" (8.5 cm) tall. If the difference is more than ¼" (6 mm), you may want to work an extra row, pull out a row, or accept that your coaster is unique and slightly different from the designer's. As long as all your squares match each other, and are an appropriate size for the coaster's function, it's fine. Remember, the edging yet to be worked will add to the dimension of the squares. If you change the number of rows, the number of stitches you work in each round of the edging will change. In that case don't be alarmed when your stitch count for the edging doesn't match the given count! When satisfied with the size and shape of the square, fasten off, leaving a tail to weave in. Weave in beginning and ending tails.

TROUBLESHOOTING/ MEASURING GAUGE

When Row 2 is complete, flatten the work without stretching and use a tape measure to check whether your 15 stitches measure 3½" (9 cm). If your row is less than 3½" (9 cm) wide, your stitches are tighter than the designer's and you should change to the next larger hook size. If your row is more than 3½" (9 cm) wide, your stitches are looser than the designer's and you should change to the next smaller hook size. By taking time to match gauge, you ensure that your project ends up the correct size and shape. This is less important with a small project such as this one, but very important when making a garment to fit a particular size body! In larger projects, it's important to work a larger gauge swatch, so that the gauge can be measured on interior stitches and rows. For a project this small, simply check that number of stitches per inch (centimeter) is reasonably close over the first couple of rows.

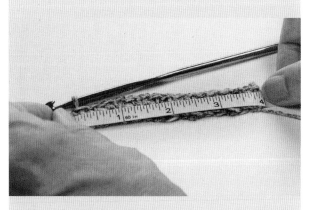

Measuring stitch gauge.

ASSEMBLY/EDGING

Make a slip knot with C and place it on the hook. Attach to the work thus: hold the two completed squares together with Row 14 of each square at the top, so the sideways Vs at the tops of the stitches have their "points" facing to the left. Insert the hook through both squares at the center of Row 14. The hook will go under the front and back loop of one A stitch and one B stitch.

Work a sc stitch by catching the working (C) yarn at the back and drawing up a loop, then completing the stitch as usual. In patterns, this step is described as, "Attach yarn C with a sc at center of row 14 of both squares, working through both thicknesses."

Edging Round 1: Work 1 sc through both thicknesses of each stitch until the corner of the piece. In corner stitch (last stitch of row 14), work 2 more sc in the same space. (Total of 3 sc in corner st. This "increase" allows the work to progress around the corner of the square.)

Now working down the side of the squares, continue to insert the hook through both thicknesses, working 1 sc in each row end, (from Row 14 to Row 1) to the next corner. Always insert the hook so that at least two strands of the row end are above the hook, to avoid stretching out the stitches. Some crocheters prefer to insert the hook under the entire end stitch of the row; some prefer to insert the hook into the side of the end stitch with two strands above the hook. It's a matter of personal preference, so try it both ways for a few stitches to see which appearance you like best. Then remove the stitches in the "other" method, and continue with the chosen method. The photograph shows insertion into the center of the row end stitches.

Hook inserted under four strands, to include a stitch from each square.

Three sts in corner.

(continued)   Working in row ends.

At next corner, work a corner increase (3 sc in same stitch). Now work along the bottom edge, inserting the hook under the remaining, unworked loop or loops of the foundation chain, through both thicknesses, matching stitches of the two squares. Work 1 sc in each ch across to corner.

Work a corner increase, in last unworked loops, then work along the row ends of Rows 1–14, as before, to final corner. Work final corner increase in the end of Row 14, then 1 sc through both thicknesses in each st to beginning of Round 1. Join the last stitch made to the first with a sl st, thus:

Insert hook under both loops of first sc, yo and pull loop through BOTH the work AND the loop on the hook, slip stitch completed.

Chain 1. Turn. {Round 1 = 62 sc, not counting slip stitch or chain}

Round 2: *Sc in each sc to corner, 3 sc in center st of corner; repeat from * 3 more times, sc in each remaining st of final side; join with a sl st. Fasten off.

Working in opposite side of chain.

Joining end of round to beginning, with a slip stitch (sl st).

CROCHET LANGUAGE

An asterisk always lets you know that a section of directions will be repeated. Follow the directions and then repeat the designated number of times by going back to the * each time you complete the direction. If directed to "repeat from * across" or "repeat from * around," then do the repeated portion over and over to the end of the current row or round.

FINISHING

Weave in yarn tails, leaving final end in the space between the two joined squares. When all four coasters are complete, steam block them.

STEAM BLOCKING TO FINISH A PROJECT

Steam blocking is a method recommended for yarns made primarily from plant fibers or synthetics, but not for wool, silk, or alpaca. Blocking methods for those fibers will be discussed later. In general, blocking is any means used to help all the stitches relax into one another, to even the tension of all the stitches, and to make the finished fabric lie flat at its correct dimensions. To block your coasters with steam, cover an ironing board or other flat surface with a terry cloth towel. Lay the coasters on the towel and use fingers to shape them into nice squares. Pin in place if they seem prone to shifting, but pinning is optional.

Lay a dampened towel over the coasters. Set the iron to its highest dry temperature setting. The moisture in the top towel will provide a more even steaming than the steam jet of the iron could. Set the hot iron gently down on the dampened upper towel. Hold in place till steam stops rising, move to the next section of towel and repeat. Pressure is not necessary, as the weight of the iron will be sufficient. Merely hold the iron in place, allowing steam to work

through the towel to the coasters. When all coasters have been steamed, turn off the iron and remove the top towel. Allow the coasters to cool and dry in place. Pins can be removed and coasters are ready to use when they are cool and dry to the touch.

TIP *The two towels are important for two reasons: they protect the texture of the crocheted fabric from becoming too flattened; and they protect the yarn from scorching in the iron's heat. Never touch a hot iron directly to crocheted fabric, regardless of fiber content!*

single crochet in rounds

Many crochet projects work best when worked "in the round." This method starts at the center of a shape and works outward in concentric rounds, just like the edging rounds of the Bright and Bold Coasters (page 38).

Crochet in the round is used for making hats, motifs, and many other items not rectangular in shape. The single crochet stitch is the same, but every round must contain the right number of increases to maintain the desired shape (flat, curving, and tubular are common shapes created by crochet in the round). The last stitch in a round connects in one of two ways with the beginning, before the next round begins. Joined rounds are the method used for the coaster edging in the last chapter. Joined rounds can be worked with turns, as in that project, or with the right side of the work facing all the time. In either case, joined rounds, like rows, always have a chain at the start, to create the height of the new stitches.

"Working in spiral," on the other hand, does not use either the slip stitch join or the starting chain. Instead, the first stitch of a new round is worked directly into the top of the first stitch of the previous round. Each method has its own advantages and limitations, which make some projects ideal for one method and some for the other. Let's start by exploring consistent increases for shaping, by making a flat circular disc as a practice swatch.

practice swatch

Flat Circle, Starting with a Ring

Start by making a slip knot and placing it on the hook. The ring will be made by creating a chain and then using a slip stitch to join the last chain to the first one made. The number of chains made to start the ring will depend on how large a hole is desired at the center of the finished piece. A hat, for instance, or the top of a doll's head, will need to be solid, without a visible hole. On the other hand, the center of an afghan square or lace tablecloth might need the open space as part of its decorative texture. Generally, a chained ring will easily hold twice as many stitches as the number of chains. Each finished shape is based on a number of stitches that "works" with its geometric construction. For instance, a circle consists of 360 degrees, geometrically. That means that the number of stitches in each should be a factor of 360—multiples of six work very well. A closed center needs to have the smallest possible multiple of six, six stitches, in Round 1, then. Knowing that the ring holds twice its stitches leads to the conclusion that the ring should start with three chains. However, a chain of only three, joined into a ring, makes it quite difficult to see the center of the ring, and misplacing the Round 1 stitches can be frustrating. A ring of four chains will still close up as the bases of the Round 1 stitches fill it, but will be easier to see and work into.

Chain 4 and join with a slip stitch, thus: insert the hook under 2 strands of the 4th ch from the hook (the first chain made, not the slip knot). Yarn over and pull that loop through the chain and through the loop on the hook, at the same time. Joining slip stitch (sl st) made.

MATERIALS

YARN
○ Worsted weight (#4)

HOOK
○ Size H (5.00 mm), I (5.50 mm), or J (6.00 mm)

NOTIONS
○ One stitch marker

SKILLS

○ How to start from a ring

○ How to space increases to make a flat circle

○ How to work joined rounds with and without turning

○ How to work spiral rounds

○ How to recognize beginning and ending of rounds, and keep track of stitch count

Joining ch 4 into a ring with sl st.

Second stitch, inserting hook in ring.

TIP *When making chains for a joined ring, work more tightly than normal. The hook will not be inserted into the actual stitches, so tightness won't be a problem. Tight chains make the center of the ring more obvious.*

Round 1: Ch 1 to start. This round will be worked by inserting the hook into the hole at the center of the ring, NOT by inserting the hook into the individual chains. This is called "working in the ring." Work 6 sc into the ring. Directions in a standard pattern will read, "6 sc in ring."

(continued)

It may be necessary, as you work around the ring, to stop after every couple of stitches and slide the completed stitches to the right, so that the ring itself is still visible to the left of the hook and so that the stitches don't overlap each other. Join final sc to first sc of the round with a sl st, in the same manner as the chains were joined in the foundation. Turn the work, just as in turning work in rows, so that the back side of Round 1 faces you.

As the circle progresses, each round must contain six increase stitches (stitches worked in the same place as another stitch) in order to keep the circle flat. This is a "rule of thumb" or formula for creating circles in single crochet. The number of necessary increases will be different when different crochet stitches are used. When finishing each round, do not work into the joining slip stitch, or the beginning chain. All work is done in the tops of the single crochet stitches. It may be helpful to place a stitch marker in the top of the first sc of each round, as soon as that stitch is completed. Slip the marker onto the loop immediately to the right of or below the hook at the completion of the stitch.

Round 2: Ch 1, work 2 sc in the first sc and in each stitch around the circle, inserting hook under both loops, just as in working in rows. At the end of Round 2, there are 12 sc. Join with a sl st to first st of the round. Turn.

Round 3: Ch 1, *2 sc in next st, sc in next sc; repeat from * around. The asterisk lets you know that a set of directions will be repeated several times. So, start by making the ch 1, and then work 2 sc in the top of the first stitch to your left. Work only 1 sc in the next stitch. Go back to the * and keep repeating that sequence till you have worked all the way around the circle. Now there are 18 stitches in the finished round. Join with a sl st. Do not turn.

Completed 3 rounds, joined and turned.

The next three rounds will be worked in joined rounds, like the first three, but without turning. This difference in method will produce a noticeably different texture in the fabric with a definite difference between the front and back, or right side and wrong side. When working into the right side (RS) of fabric, the sideways Vs at the tops of the stitches being worked in will have their points facing to the right, instead of to the left as they have when working alternating right side/wrong side rows or rounds. This may feel a bit different at first when looking for the insertion point in the top of a stitch, but is a great way to tell whether RS (right side) or WS (wrong side) of the previous row or round is facing you as you stitch.

Working into the tops of a RS round.

Round 4: Ch 1, *2 sc in next sc, sc in each of next 2 sc; repeat from * around. {24 sc}. Again, this means, notice the * and be ready to come back to it. Make 2 sc in the first stitch, and then 1 sc in the next, and 1 sc in the one after that. Now go back to the * and repeat the sequence over and over around the circle. There will be 24 sc in this round. End by joining with a sl st in first stitch of the round. Do not turn.

Completed 6 joined rounds.

Round 5: Ch 1, *2 sc in next sc, sc in each of next 3 sc; repeat from * around. Join with a sl st in first sc. {30 sc}. In other words, start as usual with 2 sc in the first stitch of the round. Work 1 sc in each of the next 3 stitches, and then repeat the sequence around the circle, ending with 30 completed sc stitches. Join the 30th stitch to the first with a slip stitch, and do not turn.

Round 6: Ch 1, *2 sc in next sc, sc in each of next 4 sc; repeat from * around. This time, do NOT join with a sl st. {36 sc}

(continued)

At this point, it's easy to see the difference in texture or surface of the two sections. The center, made from the first three joined-and-turned rounds, has an even mix between horizontal, vertical and diagonal lines in the parts of the stitches that show from either side of the work. The second section, worked from the RS without turning, looks like rings of gentle ridges on its right side, and like conjoined squares arranged in rings on the wrong side (back of the work). The next 3 rounds will have the same texture, but without the visible seam that would gradually appear if joined rounds were continued. Working in spiral, without slip stitch joins removes any visible mark where rounds end and begin. This makes for smooth shaping, but also has two other effects. It makes it difficult to keep track of the beginning of each round without a stitch marker, and it makes the beginning of the round gradually migrate in a spiral to the right, moving the distance of one stitch to the right for every round worked. Why? The top of a crochet stitch is not directly lined up over the "legs" of the stitch. This slight offset creates the spiral migration as the first stitch of each succeeding round is worked directly into the first stitch of its predecessor, without a turning or spacing chain. When working in spiral, it's essential to mark the first stitch of each round. Besides the stitch markers used so far, there is another method of marking sometimes used in this case. Cut a piece of contrasting colored yarn, 10" (25.5 cm) or so longer than you expect your whole piece to measure from center to edge. This yarn will be pulled through the first stitch in a round, and then continuously pulled through the first stitch of every successive round, forming a diagonal line across the radius of the circle. When the circle shaping is complete, the marking yarn is simply pulled out from either end.

Round 7: Insert hook under both loops of first stitch of Round 6, draw up a loop and complete the sc. Pull the marking yarn through the stitch just made. Make another sc in the same stitch. Sc in each of next 5sc, *2sc in next sc, sc in each of next 5 sc; repeat from * around. (Note that the asterisk and its repeated section are not always at the beginning of a round. When a row or round starts differently than the normal sequence of stitches, the asterisk won't appear until the first explanation of the sequence to be repeated exactly.) {42 sc}

Round 8: Sc in marked stitch, and pull marking yarn up through stitch just made, sc in same stitch and in each of next 6 sc, * 2 sc in next sc, sc in each of next 6 sc; repeat from * around. {48 sc}

Round 9: Sc in marked stitch, and pull marking yarn up through stitch just made, sc in same stitch and in each of next 7 sc, * 2sc in next sc, sc in each of next 7 sc; repeat from * around. {54 sc} To finish swatch, join last stitch of Round 9 to first stitch of Round 9 with a sl st. Fasten off. Remove marking yarn.

Marking yarn shows right-diagonal "migration" of beginning of each successive round.

TROUBLESHOOTING

It's normal for a circle in which most or all of the stitches are worked without turning to "cup" just slightly, or bend inward a little at the edges. This happens because of the structure of the sc stitch, when the RS and WS are not alternated. However, if the circle bends upward a lot, and can't be pushed flat with the fingers, it means there are too few stitches in one or more of the rows. The teal circle was started with only 5 sc in Rnd 1, instead of 6. Later, the count between increases was "accidentally" lengthened, resulting in fewer than six increases in some of the rounds. The cupping is fairly severe. Rip out a cupped circle, at least to the point where it lies flat. Check the number of stitches between increases appropriate for that round, and then continue.

On the other hand, "ruffling," as in the salmon-colored circle, is a sign that there are too many stitches in one or more rounds. This circle resulted from randomly adding occasional extra increases, as well as working in the slip stitch and turning chain in the early rounds. Rip out a ruffled circle to the point where it will lie flat, and re-work, counting to place the increases correctly and being careful NOT to crochet into the slip stitch join or the beginning chain of any round.

It will have become obvious that when all the increases are lined up with one another, the shape formed is actually a hexagon. However, a true circle can be made by simply staggering the placement of the increases from round to round. Most of the time the increase section is only a part of the whole shape, and when the rate of increase changes and the increase stitches are therefore spaced differently, the circle will "round out" and become truly round. This principle will be evident in the next project, the Roll Brim Cloche.

ROLL BRIM CLOCHE

This great hat gets its stripes from the use of a self-striping yarn. These yarns have a long run of each color, unlike a regular variegated or ombre yarn, in which each color runs for only a few inches before the next begins. As their name suggests, self-striping yarns are designed to automatically create stripes as the yarn from a single ball is used. The word "self-striping" will appear on the label, and will simplify the process of choosing an appropriate yarn. The pattern uses both spiral and joined/turned rounds for its shaping, and is also easy to adapt to other sizes. To make a child's hat, try using sport weight (#3) yarn and a G (4.25 mm) hook. For a baby or doll's hat, fingering (#2) yarn and an F (3.75 mm) hook will work. A man's hat can be made by using bulky (#5) yarn, a K (6.50–7 mm) hook, and leaving off the rolled brim.

MATERIALS

YARN

○ 200 yds (184 m) of worsted (#4) wool, wool/acrylic blend, or acrylic yarn in a self-striping colorway.

HOOK

○ Size I (5.5 mm) or hook needed to achieve gauge. Ensure proper fit by taking time to check gauge!

NOTIONS

○ Yarn needle

○ Stitch marker

GAUGE

○ Circle formed by Rnds 1–6 = 3½" (9 cm) across. Check gauge by working Rnds 1–6, then measuring diameter. If piece measures more than 3½" (9 cm) use smaller hook. If piece measures less than 3½" (9 cm) use larger hook

STITCHES AND ABBREVIATIONS USED

○ chain = ch

○ single crochet = sc

○ slip stitch = sl st

○ stitch(es) = st(s)

○ round (s) = rnd(s)

○ place marker in stitch = pm

○ move marker to new round = mm

SKILLS

○ How to use correct gauge to ensure fit for a wearable project

○ How to shape a hat using increase rounds and "work even" rounds

○ How to work "in front loop only," a single crochet variation used for shaping and texture

INSTRUCTIONS

Note: Stitch counts appear in {brackets} following instructions for the round.

Foundation: Ch 4, sl st to join in a ring.

CROWN OF HAT

Rnd 1: Ch 1, work 6 sc in ring, PM in first st made, and in each following rnd, MM to keep it always in first st of rnd. Do not join, work progresses in spiral. {6 sc}

Rnd 2: 2sc in each st around. {12 sc}

Rnd 3: *2 sc in next st, sc in next st; repeat from * around. {18 sc}

Rnd 4: *2 sc in next st, sc in each of next 2 sts; repeat from * around. {24 sc}

Rnd 5: *2 sc in next st, sc in each of next 3 sts; repeat from * around. {30 sc}

Rnd 6: *2 sc in next st, sc in each of next 4 sts; repeat from * around. {36 sc} Check gauge before proceeding.

Rnd 7: *2 sc in next st, sc in each of next 5 sts; repeat from * around. {42 sc}

Checking gauge on Rnds 1-6.

Rnd 8: *2 sc in next st, sc in each of next 6 sts; repeat from * around. {48 sc}

Rnd 9: *2sc in next st, sc in each of next 7 sts; repeat from * around. {54 sc}

Rnd 10: *2 sc in next st, sc in each of next 8 sts; repeat from * around. {60 sc}

TIP *The increase pattern changes after Rnd 10, to begin cupping the crown of the hat.*

Rnd 11: Sc in each st around. {60 sc}

Rnd 12: *2sc in next st, sc in each of next 9 sts; repeat from * around. {66 sc}

Rnd 13: Sc in each st around. {66 sc}

Rnd 14: *2sc in next st, sc in each of next 10 sts; repeat from * around. {72 sc}

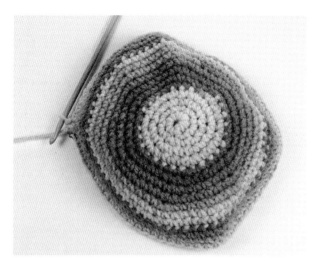

Rnds 1-16 complete.

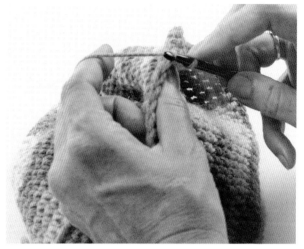

Working two rounds "in front loop only" creates a natural fold or roll for the hat's brim.

Rnd 15: Sc in each st around. {72 sc}

Piece is now slightly bowl shaped and measures 8½" to 8¾" (21.5 to 22 cm) across. Adjustment can be made by working extra rows, or ripping out a row if measurement is more than ¼" (6 mm) different.

Rnd 16: Sc in each st around. {72 sc}

SIDES OF HAT (WORKED WITHOUT INCREASE)

Rnds 17–25: Work even (that is, 1 sc in each stitch) over 72 sts. Remember to continue to MM so that the first st of each rnd is marked as that rnd is worked. At end of Rnd 25, sl st in next st, ch 1. Turn. {72 sc}

Rnd 26 (WS): Sc in each st around; join last st to first with a sl st, ch 1. Turn. {72 sc}

Rnd 27 (RS): Sc in each st around; join last st to first with a sl st, ch 1, do NOT turn.

ROLLED BRIM

Now we'll use a variation of the sc stitch, single crochet in front loop only, to shape the brim.

Rnd 28 (RS): Work 1 sc flo in each stitch around; join last st to first with a sl st, do NOT turn. {72 sc}

Rnds 29 and 30: Working in both loops, and in spiral, work 1 sc in each st around. At end of Rnd 30, sl st to join last st to first, fasten off.

FINISHING

Remove stitch marker(s). Use a large-eyed yarn needle to weave in both tails securely. To make the flowers as shown on the hat on page 50, see the instructions on page 90.

 *tell me more*

FRONT LOOP ONLY. Single crochet in front loop only, abbreviated sc flo, creates a noticeably different texture, whether used in a single row or round (for shaping) or in a whole fabric. Other than the point of insertion, this stitch is completed exactly like a regular single crochet stitch.

PHONE CARRIER

Another way to work in the round is to start with a straight chain, as if crocheting in rows. The first "row," however, works up one side of the chain, increases at the end of the chain and then works back down the opposite side. This method is very useful for creating a seamless, sturdy bottom for many types of projects—in this case, a handy carrier for a cell phone or other electronic device. Since the stitches to be used are already familiar, the new starting method, along with a new color change method, are addressed right in the context of the project.

MATERIALS

YARN
- About 75 yds (69 m) each of Color A and Color B, worsted weight acrylic or wool yarn.

HOOK
- Size G (4.25 mm) or hook needed for approximate gauge

NOTIONS
- Stitch marker
- Yarn needle

FINISHED SIZE
- Instructions are for a carrier 3½" wide by 5" tall (9 × 12.5 cm), exclusive of flap and ties. A larger carrier, suitable for an e-reader device, can be made by starting with a longer chain and working more rounds to necessary size

GAUGE
- Approximately 13 stitches = 3" (7.5 cm); approximately 14 rows = 3" (7.5 cm). Exact gauge is not necessary for this project

STITCHES AND ABBREVIATIONS USED
- chain = ch
- single crochet = sc
- slip stitch = sl st
- single crochet in back loop only = sc blo
- single crochet 2 together = sc2tog
- place marker = pm
- move marker = mm
- round(s) = rnd(s)
- stitch(es) = st(s)
- right side = RS (side facing as you stitch)
- wrong side = WS (side away from you)

SKILLS

- How to work in the round from both sides of a starting chain
- How to work single crochet in back loop only
- How to follow directions with multiple repeats
- How to change colors in continuous stitching
- How to make a simple crocheted flower
- How to make a sturdy slip stitched tie

INSTRUCTIONS

Notes:

1. Stitch counts appear in {brackets} following instructions for the round.

2. When multiple repeats are present, always work what's inside the parentheses ( ) first for the stated number of repeats and then continue with the main or asterisk (*) repeat sequence. Each time through, do the parentheses repeats first, followed by continuing the main repeat.

Foundation: With A, ch 11, loosely.

BOTTOM AND SIDES

Rnd 1: Work 3 sc in 2nd ch from hook, PM in first st made to mark beginning of rnd, sc in each of next 8 ch, 3 sc in last ch; now working in opposite side of chain, as shown in photo, sc in each of next 8 ch to complete the rnd, do not join; work proceeds in spiral. MM at beginning of each following rnd, so that first st is always easy to locate. {22 sc}

Rnd 2: *2 sc in next st, sc in next st, 2 sc in next st, sc in each of next 8 sts; repeat from * around. {26 sc}

Rnd 3: *2 sc in next st, (sc in next st, 2 sc in next st) 2 times, sc in each of next 8 sts; repeat from * around. {32 sc}

CROCHET LANGUAGE

Start the round by making 2 sc in the first stitch. Next work the sequence inside the parentheses twice, as noted by "2 times" following the parentheses. Next make 1 single crochet in each of the next 8 stitches. Now go back to the * and repeat the entire sequence, starting with the 2 sc in one st before the parentheses, next following the instructions inside the parentheses twice, and then finishing with a single crochet in each of the last 8 stitches of the round. There are now 32 sc in the completed round, and the marked first stitch is the next stitch to the left of the hook.

Working in opposite side of chain. Marker on left indicates beginning of round. Three markers in front of hook indicate points of insertion.

Point of insertion for single crochet in back loop only (sc blo)

Rnd 4: Work this round in blo. (Sc blo is very similar to the sc flo used in the last chapter. In this case, begin a stitch by inserting the hook under only the back loop at the top of the indicated stitch.) Work 1 sc blo in each stitch around, stopping just before last stitch of the round.

In last stitch of Rnd 4, change to B, thus: insert hook as usual to begin stitch. Yarn over as usual and draw up the loop to the front of the work (two loops on hook). Yarn over with the new yarn, B, and pull through both loops on hook, leaving a tail on wrong side. Cut A, leaving a 6" (15 cm) tail. For security, the tails of the two yarns can be tied together, temporarily, in a bow-knot, just like shoes. During finishing stage, the bow will be untied and each tail will be woven in to the matching-color stitches. {32 sc}

TIP *Why change colors in the final loop of a stitch? The answer lies in the structure of crochet stitches. The loop that forms the top of each stitch is actually the final loop pulled through in working the previous stitch. If colors are changed at the start of a stitch, then the loop already on the hook, when it becomes the top V of the stitch, will be a different color than the other strands making up that stitch. This discrepancy would result in an uneven appearance or "jagged edge" where colors are changed. Later, when working taller stitches, consisting of more loops, colors are always changed at the point of the final "yo and pull through 2 loops" of the last stitch in the "old" color.*

Rnds 5–22: With B and working in both loops of each st, work 1 sc in each st around. Mm to denote beginning of each round. In last stitch of Rnd 22, change to A.

WS of work, bow tied of tails.

Rnds 23 and 24: With A, sc in each st around. {32 sc}

Rnd 25: Sc in each of next 15 sts, ch 4, skip next 5 sts, sc in next st (ch-4 space made), sc in each of next 11 sts.

Rnd 26: Sc in each of next 15 sts, 5 sc in ch-4 space (just like working into a starting ring; insert hook for each stitch completely under the chain, into the large hole), sc in each of next 12 sts. Do not fasten off.

(continued)

Decrease (sc2tog).

FLAP

Work now proceeds in rows.

Row 1: Sc in each of next 9 sts of Rnd 26, ch 1. Turn, leaving remaining stitches of the rnd unworked. {9 sc}

Row 2: Sc in first st, sc2tog (see Tell Me More and photo above), sc in each of next 9 sts, sc2tog, sc in next st, ch 1. Turn. {13 sts}

Row 3: Sc in first st, sc2tog, sc in each of next 7 sts, sc2tog, sc in next st, ch 1. Turn. {11 sts}

Row 4: Sc in first st, sc2tog, sc in each of next 5 sts, sc2tog, sc in next st, ch 1. Turn. {9 sts}

tell me more

DECREASING. To decrease by working two stitches together, as in sc2tog, insert hook in first stitch as usual and draw up a loop. With 2 loops now on hook, insert hook into the next stitch and draw up a loop (3 loops now on hook). Yarn over and pull through all 3 loops on hook. The resulting stitch is two stitches wide at its base, where it's connected with the previous row, but at its top, only one stitch wide—a reduction or decrease of one stitch. In this case, a decrease near each end of the next several rows creates a diagonal shape to the sides of the flap.

Row 5: Sc in first st, sc2tog, sc in each of next 3 sts, sc2tog, sc in next st, ch 1. Turn. {7 sts}

Row 6: Sc in first st, (sc2tog, sc in next st) twice, ch 1. Turn. {5 sts}

Row 7: Sc2tog, sc in next st, sc2tog, ch 1. Turn. {3 sts}

Rows 8–10: Sc in each st, ch 1. Turn. {3 sc}

Row 11: Sc in first st, ch 10, skip next st, sc in next st (buttonloop made). Fasten off.

FLOWER BUTTON

With B, leaving an 8" tail, ch 4 and join with a sl st to form ring.

Rnd 1: Ch 1, work 9 sc in ring, sl st to join last st to first.

TIP *Remember to slide stitches to the right as you work in the ring, to prevent overlapping.*

Rnd 2: Working in front loops only, sc flo in next st, *ch 2, sc in next st; repeat from * 7 more times, ch 2, sl st in first sc. Fasten off. {9 ch-2 loops}

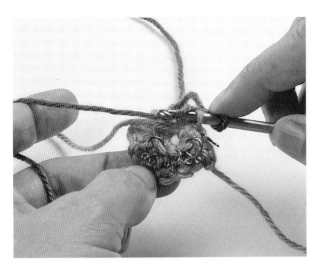

Attachment of second yarn for flower.

Rnd 3: Attach B with a sc in the unworked back loop of any stitch of Rnd 1.

All stitches of Rnd 3 are worked in remaining unworked back loops of Rnd 1. *Ch 3, sc in next st; repeat from * 7 more times, ch 3, sl st in first sc. Fasten off, leaving an 8" tail. {9 ch-3 loops}. Weave in the two shorter tails, leaving long tails to use for sewing flower to front of phone cover.

TIES
With right side facing, attach A to side of phone cover, with a sc in first unworked st of Rnd 26, beside edge of flap. Ch 45, loosely, sl st in each ch, sl st in beginning sc. Fasten off. Repeat at opposite side of flap for 2nd tie.

FINISHING
Sew flower to front center of phone carrier, 8 rows below front slit. Turn carrier inside out and weave in all ends securely. Thread end of flap through front slit, so loop of flap can fit over flower for closure. Tie ties to belt loop or strap of purse, bookbag, or diaper bag.

VARIATION
Make a carrier for an e-reader or tablet device by simply lengthening the beginning chain, and correspondingly lengthening the number of stitches between increases when making the bottom and sides. Of course, more yarn will be required and more rounds will also need to be worked before the front slit and flap. The flower can also be made in any color combination and used to embellish small accessories, such as barrettes, hair ties, zipper pulls, etc. Other and larger flower/embellishment patterns are on pages 90–91.

the double crochet stitch

The second major stitch used in crochet is the double crochet. Double crochet is a taller stitch, so every row or round worked increases the height of the fabric piece twice as fast as a row of single crochet does. Double crochet fabric is less solid, less thick, and less stiff; it drapes better and so is ideal for garments and blankets. Double crochet is also often used in combination with single crochet and other stitches to create "pattern stitches" for lace and other textures in fabric. In this chapter, we will explore the methods for making double crochet (abbreviated dc) stitches, and working them in rows and in rounds.

practice swatch

Making the Double Crochet Stitch

Start by making a swatch of sc in rows (if a review is needed, see the Practice Swatch on page 37). Work three or four rows, so there is some fabric to hold on to as the new stitch is learned. Although single crochet rows always begin with 1 chain stitch (the "turning chain"), the double crochet stitch needs a taller turning chain because it's a taller stitch. Therefore, to begin the first row of double crochet, chain 3. This is the standard turning chain for double crochet. Because the turning chain is so tall, it will actually stand in the place of the first stitch of the row. Look at your swatch and locate the first stitch in the row. Place a marker in that stitch, and place a marker in the last of the three chains just made (chain immediately below the loop on the hook).

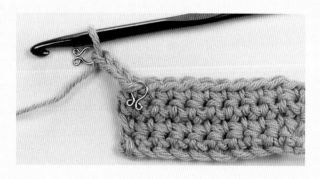

MATERIALS

YARN
∘ Worsted weight yarn

HOOK
∘ Size I (5.5 mm) or J (6 mm)

NOTIONS
∘ 3 stitch markers

SKILLS

∘ How to work the double crochet (dc) stitch with correct form and tension

∘ How to make the correct turning chain height for rows of dc

∘ How to recognize and count dc stitches and rows in a project

Turn the work, to begin the row of dc. The marked first stitch of the row will be skipped, and the first actual dc stitch of the row will be made in the stitch immediately to its left.

1 The first difference between a sc and a dc stitch is in how they are begun. The sc stitch began with insertion of the hook into the designated stitch. The dc stitch, however, begins with a yarn over (yo). This is done in the same direction as all yarn overs, back to front, right to left, with the yarn coming over the top of the hook and down in front of it.

Now insert the hook in the second stitch of the row (left of the marker), yo at the back of the work (a) and draw up a loop. There are now three loops on the hook (b).

2 Yarn over and pull that new loop through the first two loops on the hook. This step is designated "yo and pull through 2."

3 There are still two loops on the hook. Yo again, and pull the loop through the two remaining on the hook. A double crochet stitch is completed.

4 To make the second stitch, repeat steps 1–3, inserting the hook in the next stitch in the row.

Yo, insert hook, and draw up a loop.

Yo and pull through 2.

Yo and pull through 2.

5 Continue across the row, till one dc stitch stands in each sc stitch of the previous row. Now move the marker from the skipped stitch at the beginning of the row, and place it in the last stitch of the row, the last stitch made. This will be the skipped stitch at the beginning of the next row. Chain 3, mark the 3rd chain made, and turn the work.

(continued)

Working Rows of Double Crochet

The second and all following rows begin in the same way as the first: with a ch-3 to turn, skipped first stitch, and then 1 dc in each stitch of the row. As soon as the first stitch of Row 2 is made, remove the marker from the skipped stitch, to use again in a few moments. When the second row is nearly complete, the last stitch of the row will be made into the marked 3rd chain of the previous row's turning chain. In this way, the number of stitches stays the same from row to row and each turning chain "becomes" a dc stitch.

As usual, there are several ways to insert into the chain, but the best appearance of the stitch will be achieved by inserting the hook beneath the front loop and bottom bump. Since the back of that row is facing, these are the top two strands facing you as you look at the turning chain.

Markers show top of turning chain and location of last stitch of Row 2.

Hook inserted beneath front loop and bottom bump of chain.

Completed 2nd row.

practice swatch #2

Double Crochet Worked into Chain

Many projects begin with a row of double crochet stitches worked directly into the starting chain. Because each row of double crochet must start with a turning chain as tall as the stitches themselves, the beginning chain must be three chain stitches longer than the number of stitches required (for the turning chain), and then that turning chain will count as the first stitch of the first row of double crochet. This creates a net difference of two stitches. When working rows of single crochet, the length of the starting chain was one more than the desired number of stitches—eleven chains to make a swatch with ten stitches per row. To make ten stitches per row in double crochet, the starting chain will be twelve stitches.

Practice making dc in a longer chain, remembering to do a yarn over at the beginning of each stitch, before inserting the hook into the next chain. When the process is comfortable and consistent, you're ready to make the "Longitude Scarf," which will use rows of both single and double crochet!

Ch 12, dc in 4th ch from hook and in each ch across.

There are now nine actual dc stitches and a ch-3 that counts as a stitch, making a total of ten stitches in the row.

COUNTING STITCHES AND ROWS

Like the single crochet stitches you're familiar with, each double crochet stitch has a sideways "V" at the top. When the right side of the completed stitches is facing, the Vs all point to the right. When the work has been turned and the wrong side of completed stitches is facing, the Vs point to the left. Stitches in a row can be counted by counting the Vs. However, remember that the first stitch of each row is actually the turning chain, and it has a slightly different appearance. The V is there, but is a little more difficult to see clearly. Many people find it easier to count their dc stitches by looking at the vertical part of the stitch, called the post. Each post has a diagonal twist on the right side, and a series of knots on the wrong side. Each post stands just below and slightly to the left of its V-shaped top. It's easy to see that the turning chain creates a vertical post like all the others in a row.

Work several more rows of dc, using the markers for last stitch in each row (first skipped stitch in the following row) and for the top of the turning chain (3rd chain made), where the last stitch of the following row will be placed. At the end of each row, count to make sure there are still ten stitches. Use the Troubleshooting box to make sure your stitches are the correct height and shape, that is, that your tension is neither too tight nor too loose. When the process becomes familiar, proceed to the second practice swatch, in which dc stitches will be worked directly into a starting chain.

Each swatch shows 10 rows of work—4 rows of blue sc, 2 rows of pink sc, and 4 rows of green dc. Left: Right side of Row 1 is facing. Yellow pins mark tops of Rows 1, 3, 5, 7, and 9. Right: Wrong side of Row 1 is facing, pink pins mark tops of Rows 2, 4, 6, 8, and 10.

TROUBLESHOOTING

Most problems with double crochet in rows are caused by a few common errors. The most common mistakes are shown here, for comparison with your swatch.

Swatch on left shows the gradual increase in stitch count caused by NOT skipping the first stitch as each row begins. Swatch on right shows gradual decrease in stitch count caused by NOT working the last stitch of each row in the top of the turning ch-3.

Left—Stitches much too loose, tangling and collapsing on themselves.

Right—Stitches short and "squat," no taller than sc, caused by yanking or tugging the yarn to tighten after each "yo and pull through 2 loops" step in each stitch.

LONGITUDE SCARF

With looped chain fringe and bold lengthwise stripes, this cozy scarf pattern makes great gifts for men, women, and kids.

MATERIALS

YARN

∘ Worsted weight (#4) wool or acrylic yarn, approx. 109 yds (100.3 m) of A, approx. 150 yds of B

HOOKS

∘ J (6.00 mm) and I (5.50 mm) or hooks needed to obtain gauge

NOTIONS

∘ Stitch markers (optional) for row ends and turning chains

∘ Large-eyed yarn needle

GAUGE

∘ In dc stitches with smaller hook, 9 sts = 3" (7.5 cm) and 2 rows = 1½" (4 cm). However, exact gauge is not necessary for this project

FINISHED SIZE

∘ 5½" wide by 58" long (14 × 147.5 cm), including fringe

STITCHES AND ABBREVIATIONS USED

∘ chain = ch

∘ single crochet = sc

∘ double crochet = dc

∘ slip stitch = sl st

∘ stitch(es) = st(s)

∘ yarn over = yo

SKILLS

∘ How to carry yarn from one row to another when making stripes

∘ How to change yarn colors in double crochet

∘ How to attach a new ball of yarn when the ball in use runs out

∘ How to make looped chain fringe

∘ How to combine single crochet and double crochet stitches in one project

INSTRUCTIONS

Notes:

1. Stitch counts appear in {brackets} at the ends of rows.

2. Turning ch-3 counts as a dc at beginning of all dc rows. Turning ch-1 does NOT count as a sc at beginning of all sc rows. If necessary, mark first stitch of each row.

3. Scarf can be made longer or shorter by modifying number of ch in foundation. Add or subtract 3 ch per inch of modification desired.

Foundation: With larger hook and A, chain 151.

TIP *To count large numbers of chain stitches accurately, place a stitch marker every 25 stitches or so. Remove the markers as Row 1 is worked.*

SCARF

Row 1: Change to smaller hook, sc in bottom bump of 2nd ch from hook and in each ch across. In last stitch, change to B, see explanation on pages 56 and 57. {150 sc}

Row 2: With B, ch 3 (in addition to loop that created color change), counting turning ch as first stitch, dc in each stitch across. {150 dc}

Row 3: Ch 3, dc in each stitch across, changing to A in last stitch. Be sure not to pull too tightly on A in the color change. Leave sufficient yarn for the "carry" to lie flat across the ends of the rows without curling the piece as it's worked. {150 dc}

TIP *To change colors in a dc stitch, begin with the old color. Yo and insert hook into designated stitch, yo and draw up a loop (3 loops on hook). Yo and pull through 2 loops (2 loops remain on hook). Yo with new color and pull through both loops on hook. In a striped project, such as this one, DON'T cut the first color! Let it hang until it's needed again in a few rows. At that time, simply pick it up with the hook when ready to "yo with new color."*

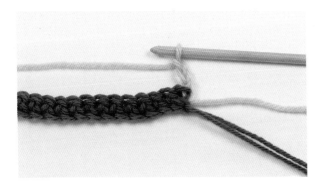

TIP *Attaching a new ball of yarn—At some point in the project, the first ball of B is likely to be used up. When this happens, attach the new yarn just as if it were a new color: with 6" (15 cm) or so of the old yarn remaining, work the first half of the next stitch. Finish the stitch by doing the final "yo and pull through" with the new yarn. The two yarn tails can be temporarily tied together in a bow, and woven in during finishing of the project.*

Row 4: With A, ch 1, sc in each st across, ch 1. Turn. {150 sc}

Row 5: Sc in each st across. In last stitch, change to B.

Rows 6 and 7: Repeat Rows 2 and 3.

Rows 8 and 9: Repeat Rows 4 and 5.

Rows 10 and 11: Repeat Rows 2 and 3.

Row 12: Repeat Row 4. At end of Row 12, fasten off B.

LOOPED CHAIN FRINGE

Row 1: With A, ch 1, rotate piece to work in row ends, sc in each sc row end and 2 sc in each dc row end (work over the strands of yarn carried from one stripe to another, to hide them). Fasten off A. At opposite end of scarf, attach A and repeat this row. {18 sc at each end of scarf}

Row 2: Sc in first st of Row 1, *ch 24, sc in next st; repeat from * across. Fasten off. Repeat at other end of scarf. {17 loops}

FINISHING

Use large-eyed yarn needle to weave in all ends securely.

double crochet motifs in living color

Many crochet projects, both traditional and current, are constructed of small pieces, or motifs, attached to one another in decorative patterns, which create a highly graphic fabric. The variety in motifs, from simple to amazingly complex, is almost infinite. They are made in many shapes and sizes, can use one color or several, and can be joined to create anything from tablecloths to clothing and accessories. However, they do all have a few things in common. All motifs are worked from the center outward, and all use careful placement of the increases to create their shapes.

Let's explore some variations and uses of the most famous of crochet motifs—the "granny square." The classic granny square motif consists of groups of double crochet stitches (usually 3 or 4 stitches per group) separated by chain spaces. Each round is worked in the chain spaces of the previous round, and the corners are formed by working two groups of stitches and their separating space in one corner space. The granny square was very popular during the late 1960s and the 1970s, and is enjoying a resurgence of popularity in the second decade of the twenty-first century. It's one of those classic designs that cycles into "current fashion" at least once in each generation. So grab a familiar hook and a couple of balls of worsted yarn in colors you love, and let's get going with grannies!

practice swatch A

Basic Granny Square in One Color– 4 Rounds

Start with ch 4, and slip stitch to join in a ring.

Rnd 1: Ch 3 (counts as first dc), work 2 dc in ring, then make a corner increase by working ch 2, (3 dc in ring, ch 2) 3 times, join last ch with a sl st in top of beginning ch 3. At the end of the rnd, there are 4 groups of 3 dc, separated by ch-2 spaces.

TIP *Be sure the sl st that finishes the round is made IN the top of the ch-3, not AROUND it. Inserting the hook under the chain and working around it will create an extra space in the stitching, which will seriously affect the finished appearance of the piece, and may also lead to difficulties in determining where stitches should be placed in the following round.*

Rnd 2: Ch 4 (counts as dc and ch-1), place marker in 3rd ch of the ch-4, skip next group of dc, (3 dc, ch 2, 3 dc) in next ch-2 space. This sequence in parentheses will be repeated at every corner throughout the granny square, no matter how many rounds are made.

The corner increase to keep the square flat and correctly shaped is made by working this sequence in each of the four corners of each round. Many patterns, having thus explained the corner increase one time, will, in following rounds, simply say, "Make corner." This is especially true in older patterns.

MATERIALS

YARN
- Worsted yarn in three colors (light, medium, and dark)

HOOK
- Size H (5 mm) or I (5.5 mm)

NOTIONS
- One stitch marker

SKILLS

- How to make square motifs by careful placement of corner increases
- Working in chain spaces instead of in stitches
- How to make a "granny square" of any size and color sequence

Completed Rnd 1, correctly joined.

Round 2, started and first corner worked.

Completing Rnd 2.

*Ch 1, skip next 3-dc group, work corner increase (that is, 3 dc, ch 2, 3 dc) in next ch-2 space; repeat from * one time, ch 1, skip next 3-dc group, (3 dc, ch 2, 2 dc) in last ch-2 space, sl st to join in marked 3rd ch of beginning ch-4. Again, be sure to work into and not around the chain.

Rnd 3: Sl st into ch-1 space, ch 3, 2 dc in same ch-1 space.

*Ch 1, (3 dc, ch 2, 3 dc) in next ch-2 space, ch 1, 3 dc in next ch-1 space; repeat from * twice more (3 corners formed), ch 1, (3 dc, ch 2, 3 dc) in last ch-2 space, ch 1, sl st to join in top of beginning ch-3.

(continued)

Beginning Rnd 3.

Rnd 4: Ch 4, place marker in 3rd ch made, 3 dc in next ch-1 space, ch 1, work corner in next ch-2 space, *ch 1, 3 dc in next ch-1 space*; repeat between * and * to next corner ch-2 spaced, work corner in ch-2 space; repeat between * and * to next corner, repeat entire sequence of side and corner around, ending with 2 dc in last ch-1 space, sl st to join in marked 3rd ch of beginning ch-4. Fasten off.

OPTIONAL EDGING ROUND

Attach a second color, with a sc in any ch-1 (side) space. Work 1 sc in each dc and 1 sc in each ch-space to next corner. Work (2 sc, ch 1, 2 sc) in corner. Repeat sides and corners around, ending with a sl st to join last st to first stitch. Fasten off.

TIP *Locating the top of the first stitch in a 3-dc group—Remember that the top of any crochet stitch is slightly offset from its vertical stem or post. When alternating between working in a space and working in the first stitch after the space, look for the V at the top and slightly to the right of the first stitch in the next group.*

Completing Rnd 3.

Complete through Rnd 4.

Sometimes it's a little difficult to locate the top of the first stitch after a space!

Optional edging.

TROUBLESHOOTING—COMMON GRANNY SQUARE MISTAKES

When a granny square "goes wrong," it's usually because of one or more of the following common mistakes. In each case, the work needs to be ripped out to the point where the mistake occurred. Because of the way each round builds on the previous one, it doesn't work to try to adjust the number of stitches inan outer round, if the inner ones are "off."

Mistake #1—If the first round contains 3 or 5 groups of 3 dc, the resulting shape will not be a square, and the increases won't be correct for keeping it flat. Swatch on left shows result of 5 dc groups in Rnd 1; swatch on right shows result of 3 dc groups in Rnd 1.

Mistake #2—If the joining sl st at the ends of rounds is worked around instead of into the chain, a hole results, and in a following round, it's then easy to interpret that hole as a ch-1 or ch-2 space needing to be worked in. This results in too many 3-dc groups on the side where rounds begin and end. Markers show slip stitches worked around the beginning chain.

Mistake #3—This square lost a corner, at the marked spot, because there's only one 3-dc group in the corner space, instead of the proper corner increase.

practice swatch B

Traditional Three- Color Granny Square

Call your lightest chosen color A; the medium color B, and the darkest color C.

With A, work foundation chain and ring, the same as in Swatch #1.

Rnd 1: Work as in first square (page 71). At end of Rnd 1, fasten off A.

Rnd 2: Attach B with a dc in any corner ch-2 space.

TIP *Attaching a new yarn with a dc—Place a slip knot of the new color on the hook. Yo before inserting hook into indicated stitch or space. Insert the hook and complete the stitch as usual. This method minimizes the number of places in a piece that a ch-3 has to stand for a dc—since that's functional, but never looks quite right. This method is also invisible, no slip stitch to show where the new yarn was attached!*

Complete that corner, ch 1, *skip next 3-dc group, work corner, ch 1; repeat from * around, ending with sl st in first dc.

Rnd 3: Ch 4 (counts as dc and ch 1), mark 3rd ch made, skip to next corner ch-2 space, work corner, ch 1, *3 dc in next ch-1 space, ch 1, corner in ch-2 corner space; repeat from * until all 4 corners are worked, 2 dc in last ch-1 space, join with a sl st to marked ch of beginning ch 3. Fasten off B.

Rnd 4: Attach C with a dc in any ch-2 corner space (counts as first dc of corner). Complete the corner, ch 1, work around in pattern, working (3 dc, ch 1) in each ch-1 space on the sides of the square, and (3 dc, ch 2, 3 dc) in each corner ch-2 space, end with ch 1,sl st to join to first dc of round. Fasten off C. Weave in all yarn ends, into matching color yarn.

Optional edging round: A sc edging around each granny can make joining several squares easier and more attractive. It's also an effective tool in the color scheme. Try using A again to edge the completed square, as in Practice Square A.

Now that both single-color and multi-color granny squares are familiar, they can be made in different sizes, and combined into a variety of projects!

TROUBLESHOOTING—THE LOGIC OF GRANNY SQUARES

Some people find granny squares confusing because of the alternating nature of the stitch pattern's repetitions. If you're simply following one instruction after another, it's hard to understand why sometimes the round starts with ch 3, counting as the first stitch of the round, but sometimes starts with ch 4, which will stand as the last stitch of the round! If only following a series of separate instructions, it's difficult to see why sometimes there's a ch-1 space, and sometimes there's a ch-2 space! But if the "big picture" is kept in view, it all becomes clear. The granny square is really an exercise in logic, a series of "if-then" statements:

IF the round begins with a space immediately to the left of the sl st join,

THEN ch 3 and work in that space; it's the next possible place to make a 3-dc group.

IF the round begins with a space immediately to the right of the sl st join,

THEN, ch 4, and skip to the next place where a 3-dc group can be worked. Work always progresses around the square moving to the left.

IF the space being worked is on the side of the square,

THEN it's a ch-1 space. All three stitches of the dc group will fit in that space. More chains on a straight side would create "ruffles" as we saw earlier in learning to increase keeping a shape flat.

IF the space being worked is on a corner of the square,

THEN it's a ch-2 space. Since two whole 3-dc groups will have to be worked into that space, it needs to be wider than a "side" space, to accommodate the greater number of stitches. It also takes more chains to work around the corner (increasing) than to work along a straight side.

GRAB-AND-GO GRANNY BAG

Whether used for books, groceries, or skeins of yarn, this versatile and spacious bag is a great accessory! The bag is made from two sizes of granny squares and a larger square that's a solid stitch variation on the granny square theme. The sample is shown in a warm and muted color scheme, but the project would look equally great in cool, clear jewel tones, or neon brights. Or feel free to use your imagination and what you've learned about confident color choices!

MATERIALS

YARN

- 1 skein each of 5 colors (A, light, 300 yds [276 m]; B and D medium solids 100 yds [92 m]; C dark solid 100 yds [92 m]; E, variegated or space-dyed in a related color 200 yds [184 m])

HOOK

- Size H (5 mm) or size needed to obtain gauge

NOTIONS

- One stitch marker
- Large-eyed yarn needle

GAUGE

- Completed Round 1 of each motif measures 1½" to 1¾" (3.8 to 4.5 cm) from side to side. However, exact gauge is not essential for this project

FINISHED SIZE

- 12½" (32 cm) square; strap is 3½" wide by 40" (9 × 103 cm) long

STITCHES AND ABBREVIATIONS USED

- chain = ch
- slip stitch = sl st
- single crochet = sc
- double crochet = dc
- stitch(es) = st(s)
- round = rnd
- single crochet 2 together (decrease) = sc2tog (see instructions in Project 4)
- special stitch = corner (3 dc, ch 2, 3 dc)

SKILLS

- How to connect individual motifs by three different methods
- How to make a solid stitch motif, a variation on the granny square theme

INSTRUCTIONS

Notes:

1. Stitch counts for rounds appear in {brackets} following round instructions.

2. All rounds of each square are worked with right side facing.

FIRST SIDE OF BAG

1 Make 4 medium granny squares following instructions below. Each square begins with A at center. Rnds 2–4 are worked with one of the contrast colors: B, C, D, and E. Final round is worked with A.

With A, ch 4, sl st to join in a ring.

Rnd 1: Ch 3, 2 dc in ring, ch 2, *3 dc in ring, ch 2; repeat from * twice more, join last ch in top of beginning ch-3 with a sl st. Fasten off A. {Four 3-dc groups, 4 ch-2 corner spaces}

Rnd 2: Attach contrast color with a dc in any corner ch-2 space, (2 dc, ch 2, 3 dc) in same space, ch 1, *skip next 3 dc, work corner in next ch-2 space (see special stitch, above), ch 1; repeat from * around, ending with sl st to join last ch to first dc of rnd. {Eight 3-dc groups, 4 ch-1 spaces on sides of square, 4 ch-2 spaces at corners}

Rnd 3: Ch 4, mark 3rd ch made, skip next 3-dc group, *work corner in next ch-2 space, ch 1, skip 3 dc, 3 dc in next ch-1 space, ch 1; repeat from * around, 2 dc in last ch-1 space, sl st to join in marked 3rd ch of beginning ch-4. {Twelve 3-dc groups, 4 ch-2 spaces at corners, 8 ch-1 spaces along sides}

Rnd 4: Sl st into ch-1 space immediately to the left of join just made, ch 3, 2 dc in same ch-1 space, ch 1, skip to next ch-2 space, *work corner in ch-2 space, ch 1, 3 dc in next ch-1 space, ch 1, 3 dc in next ch-1 space, ch 1; repeat from * around, ending with ch 1, sl st to join last ch in top of beginning

ch-3. Fasten off. {Sixteen 3-dc groups, 4 ch-2 spaces at corners, and 12 ch-1 spaces along sides}.

Rnd 5: Attach A with a dc in any corner ch-2 space, (dc, ch 2, 2 dc) in same ch-2 space, *dc in each st and in each ch-1 space to next corner, work (2 dc, ch 2, 2 dc) in corner ch-2 space. {19 dc along each side, and 4 ch-2 spaces at corners}. Note that the corners are slightly different on this round of solid stitching! Fasten off and weave in all yarn tails.

2 Join four granny squares with a whip stitch seam. Hold two squares with wrong sides together, so that right side of work faces outward on both sides.

Thread about an arm's length of A onto large-eyed yarn needle. Leaving at least 8" (20.5 cm) of tail, insert the needle under one arm of the V at the top of the first stitch of the first square, AND under one arm of the V at the top of the first stitch of the second square. The seam will look neatest if needle is inserted under the "inner" strands, the two touching each other as the squares are held together. Pull the yarn through, making sure to leave tail still hanging. Holding the two squares together so that corners and spaces match, match the stitches from the two squares and continue with the next pair of stitches: insert needle from the same side as the first whip-stitch, pull through, insert from same direction in next pair of stitches, all the way across the row. All stitches are made with the needle pointed in the same direction, although which direction that is will depend on what's comfortable for each stitcher. Some prefer to push the needle toward themselves; while some prefer to push the needle away. As long as all stitches in the row are consistent, the result will be the same.

When the first two squares are joined, fasten off yarn and weave in the beginning and ending tail of the seam. Repeat the process for the second pair

of squares, again making sure that the right side of the work faces outward, so that you're looking at the same side of the square as while crocheting it. Now hold the two rectangles in the same manner and sew a longer seam, starting with nearly two arms' length of yarn to ensure that it's enough for weaving in tails. When all four squares are joined, work edging.

3 **Edging for First Side. Rnd 1:** Attach D with a sc in any ch-2 space, with right side of work facing, work 2 more sc in same ch-2 space, *sc in every st along side to next ch-2 space, working 1 sc in each ch-1 space and 1 sc in end of seam, 3 sc in next ch-2 space; repeat from * around, joining final st to first st with a sl st. {41 sc along each side and 3 sc in each corner}. Weave in all remaining yarn tails and set first side of bag aside.

SECOND SIDE OF BAG

4 Make one large motif as follows: With A, ch 4, sl st to join in ring.

Rnd 1: Work as Rnd 1 for medium granny square above, but DO NOT fasten off at completion of rnd. {Four 3-dc groups}

Rnd 2: Ch 3, dc in each of next 2 sts, *(2 dc, ch 2, 2 dc) corner in next ch-2 space (notice that this is a slightly different corner from that used in the granny squares), dc in each of next 3 sts; repeat from * around, ending with (2 dc, ch 2, 2 dc) in last ch-2 space, join last st to top of beginning ch-3 with a sl st. Fasten off A, leaving long enough tail to weave in securely. {7 dc on each side of square}

Rnd 3: Attach B with a dc in first st to the left of any corner ch-2 space. *dc in each st to next ch-2 space, (2 dc, ch 2, 2 dc) in ch-2 space; repeat from * around, ending with sl st to join last st of last corner with first st of rnd. {11 dc on each side of square}

Rnd 4: Ch 3, *dc in each st to next ch-2 space, work corner in ch-2 space; repeat from * around, ending with dc in each of last 2 sts; sl st to join. Fasten off B. {15 dc per side of square}

Rnd 5: Attach C with a dc in first dc to the left of any ch-2 space. Work same as Rnd 3. {19 dc per side of square}

Rnd 6: Work same as Rnd 4. At end of rnd, fasten off C. {23 dc per side}

Rnd 7: With E (instead of B), work same as Rnd 3. {27 dc per side}

Rnd 8: Work same as Rnd 4. Fasten off E. {31 dc per side}

Rnd 9: With A, work same as Rnd 3. {35 dc per side}

Rnd 10: Work same as Rnd 4. Fasten off A. {39 dc per side}

Rnd 11: With D, work same as Rnd 3. Fasten off D. {43 dc per side}.

(continued)

Weave in all yarn tails securely into matching color yarn areas. If stitch counts are correct, the stitches of the edge of this motif will match the edging stitches of completed first side of bag. (The corner sc of the first side "matches" the ch-2 space of the second side). Set completed second side of bag aside.

STRAP

5 Make 12 small motifs following instructions below.

Beginning, Rnds 1 and 2: With E, follow directions for Rnds 1 and 2 of large motif. Fasten off. {7 dc per side}

Rnd 3: Attach A with a sc in first st to left of any ch-2 space, *sc in each st to next ch-2 space, 4 sc in ch-2 space; repeat from * around, ending with a sl st to join last sc to first sc of rnd. Fasten off. Weave in tails.

6 **Assemble Strap.** Hold 2 small squares with wrong sides together and edge stitches aligned. Working through all 4 loops (both loops of edge stitches of each square) attach A at right hand edge and work 11 sl sts across.

Repeat sl st seam till all 12 motifs are joined, end to end, in a long line. When complete, weave in all yarn tails securely.

7 **Strap Edging.** Attach D with a sc in st at right hand edge of either short end of strap, *sc in each st across to corner, ch 1, rotate to work along long side of strap, sc in each st of long side, also working 1 sc in end of each seam, ch 1, rotate and repeat from * one more time. Join last stitch to first with a sl st. Fasten off D and weave in tails.

ASSEMBLE BAG

8 **Crochet Bag Front and Back Together.** Hold first and second sides of bag together, with wrong sides together and right sides facing outward. Attach D with a sc through both loops of both pieces at any corner, *sc in each st across, matching sts of both sides, and working through both loops of each side (inserting hook under 4 loops to begin each st) to next corner, 3 sc in corner; repeat from * 2 more times until 3 sides of the bag are crocheted together, on 4th, open, side, work through only 1 thickness (inserting hook under only 2 loops of one side of bag for each st), sc in each st across one side of bag, turn bag and work 1 sc in each st across other side of bag, join final sc to first sc of rnd with a sl st, ch 1 and continue in same direction, working another rnd of sc across open top of bag, join with a sl st. Fasten off.

9 **Attach Strap to Bag.** Position one short end of stap inside top edge of bag with wrong sides together, so that the 12 sts of strap match last 12 sts of bag top edging. With D, sl st through both pieces, matching sts, across. Fasten off. Repeat with opposite end of strap and opposite side of bag.

TIP *Slip Stitch Seam—Working a series of slip stitches is another way to join motifs or other pieces of crocheted fabric together. As with any other slip stitch, insert the hook through the indicated loops or stitches, draw up a loop to the front and immediately through the loop on the hook. Make sure to pull the loop through far enough that the resulting stitch is not too tight. Extra tight slip stitch seams will cause puckering of the work. The seam should appear on the right side of the work as a flat triple-braid.*

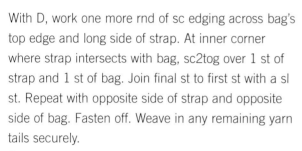

With D, work one more rnd of sc edging across bag's top edge and long side of strap. At inner corner where strap intersects with bag, sc2tog over 1 st of strap and 1 st of bag. Join final st to first st with a sl st. Repeat with opposite side of strap and opposite side of bag. Fasten off. Weave in any remaining yarn tails securely.

TIP *The Right Seam for the Job—In this project we've used three different seaming methods. Other methods also exist, and some of them will be covered later. Generally, a stitcher may choose his or her favorite method, and many patterns will merely direct, "seam pieces together." The seam methods for this project were chosen because of their differing characteristics for different structural functions. The whip stitch that joined the four grannies of the first side, is a nearly invisible seam when sewn carefully, matching stitches. However, the seam is only one strand thick, and so is not as sturdy as some others. It was chosen because this area of the bag is not in much danger of stretching or being otherwise stressed, and the invisible nature of the seam means that the eye's attention is on the colors of the granny squares, rather than on the seam. The slip stitch seams of the strap were chosen because a strap needs to be both flat and very sturdy. A slip stitch seam is NOT invisible, but is rather decorative, and the motifs being joined were fairly plain. The slip stitch seam is also very strong, and also doesn't cause a ridge, which might irritate a shoulder if the bag is full and heavy! The single crochet seam of the bag's outer edges was chosen because it creates both a decorative ridged edging, and puts the largest number of strands of yarn in the place where the seam will receive the most structural stress. So, when working other projects, and choosing your own seaming method, keep in mind the function and appearance of the seamed area, and choose the best seam for the job!*

PUTTING IT TOGETHER

The lessons learned in this section will build on your basic skills and give you confidence as you choose projects to crochet. You will be introduced to the international stitch symbols for crochet and learn how to interpret them to follow instructions. Your crochet horizons will be expanded as you learn more basic stitches and discover interesting stitch patterns and textures that develop from using combinations of stitches over several rows.

combining stitches, reading charts

Crochet is truly an international art, with deep cultural roots in many areas of both Asia and Europe. Today, designers from Brazil, Russia, Ukraine, Japan, Korea, Western Europe, and North America can all communicate patterns and instructions by using a set of international stitch symbols.

It might be intimidating to take on the entire array of symbols, especially since the stitches they represent haven't been taught yet! The chart below shows some of the more common symbols you will encounter. Let's start with the stitches we've learned. You already know what the actual stitch looks like in your work, and you know their names and the abbreviations that describe them in a pattern. It's only one more step to recognize the graphic symbol for each:

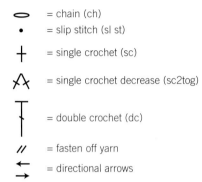

= chain (ch)
= slip stitch (sl st)
= single crochet (sc)
= single crochet decrease (sc2tog)
= double crochet (dc)
= fasten off yarn
= directional arrows

STITCH SYMBOL KEY

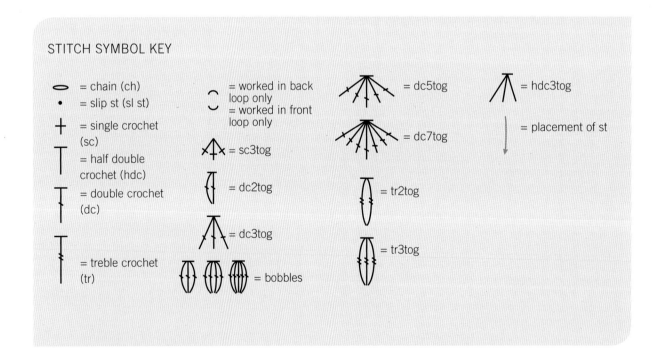

= chain (ch)
= slip st (sl st)
= single crochet (sc)
= half double crochet (hdc)
= double crochet (dc)
= treble crochet (tr)

= worked in back loop only
= worked in front loop only
= sc3tog
= dc2tog
= dc3tog
= bobbles

= dc5tog
= dc7tog
= tr2tog
= tr3tog

= hdc3tog
= placement of st

practice swatch #1

MATERIALS

YARN
○ About 10 yds (9.15 m) of scrap yarn, worsted weight

HOOK
○ Size H (5 mm)

SKILLS

○ How to read a simple stitch diagram in rows

○ How to create a swatch from a stitch symbol diagram

When we read written English, we read from left to right, but this is not necessarily the direction of movement in reading a symbol diagram. In diagrams, what matters is the direction of the stitching. When working in rows, we turn the work so that every row is worked from right to left, but if the right side of the fabric is facing, then one row is stitches whose top-V's face left, and the next is a row whose top-V's face to the right, back and forth from row to row. This is the way stitch diagrams are read when the work is in rows.

Follow the diagram, as explained in the caption, and make the swatch. If you find yourself "stuck," here is the written pattern in familiar abbreviated English form:

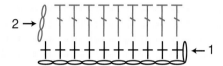

Read the diagram starting at the bottom left. The chains progress across the bottom. The last chain is at an angle, showing that its function is the "turning chain." Row 1 is read from right to left. The number "1" is at the side where the eye should start reading. Row 2, read from left to right, has its beginning chain at its start, and the number "2" stands at the beginning of the row. The diagram is read by understanding that each symbol is a little picture of an individual stitch.

Foundation: Ch 11, turn.

Row 1: Sc in 2nd ch from hook and each ch across. Turn. {10 sc}

Row 2: Ch 3, dc in 2nd stitch and each st across. Fasten off.

Here's the finished swatch:

practice swatch #2

Rounds

When working in rounds, the diagram is read from where the crochet begins: the center, moving outward, just as the crochet rounds progress outward from the center.

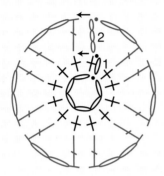

Start reading at the center, counting the chain symbols. The slip stitch symbol notes where the next round will begin. The next round is printed in a different color in this and many other diagrams.

The symbols for the stitches of Round 1 don't line up exactly over the chain symbols, because as in most motifs, the single crochets are being worked into the ring, and there are more stitches in Round 1 than in the foundation ring. Count the symbols for sc to see how many stitches to work. Most motifs are worked with right side facing, as were our motifs in Chapter 6. If a circle diagram wants you to turn the work and work in the opposite direction, a little arrow will direct you at the beginning of a round. In this case, the direction doesn't change, so proceed with right side of Round 1 still facing, working in the same direction. Round 2 begins with chains, and then each dc symbol is standing directly on top of the stitch into which it should be worked. Here's the written pattern, in case you need to refer to it—but you'll gain diagram skill most quickly by trying to "see" the stitches in the diagram first and only referring to the written words when really necessary.

MATERIALS

YARN
○ About 10 yds (9.15 m) of scrap yarn, worsted weight

HOOK
○ Size H (5 mm)

SKILLS

○ How to read a symbol diagram for crochet in rounds

○ How to create a small motif from a symbol diagram

Foundation: Ch 6, join with sl st to form ring.

Rnd 1: Ch 1, work 12 sc in ring; join last st to first with a sl st.

Rnd 2: Ch 3, dc in next st, ch 2, *dc in each of next 2 sts, ch 2; repeat from * around, ending with sl st in top of beginning ch-3. Fasten off. {12 dc and 6 ch-2 spaces}

Here's the resulting swatch:

practice swatch #3

Here's a stitch symbol diagram version of the pattern for the 3-color granny square made as Practice Swatch B on page 74. Try following the diagram without looking back at the written directions. Color changes are shown by the use of different colored ink in the diagram. When finished, the square should be the same as the one already made.

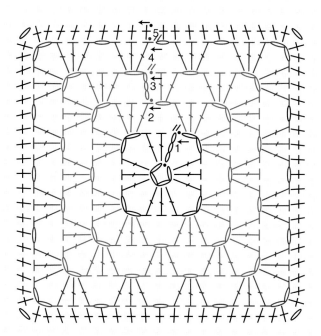

MATERIALS

YARN

○ Approximately 25 yds (23 m) scrap worsted yarn in each of two colors, A and B

HOOK

○ Size H (5 mm)

SKILLS

○ More practice in following a multiround diagram

○ How to make the familiar granny square without written directions

FLOWER POWER RETRO BEANIE

Now that some of the mystery of symbol diagrams has been removed, it's time to make a whole project by following these international symbols. Many crocheters find that this becomes their preferred pattern type. Others always lean toward written word/abbreviation directions, but both groups benefit from being able to refer to the "other" set of directions when in doubt as to meaning in the pattern being followed.

The Flower Power Hat will give you opportunity to practice following stitch symbol diagrams, while also offering the word directions. For now, it's probably best to start this project with the smaller flowers,

made from simpler diagrams, and then make the motifs, following the more complex diagram. The motifs in this project are similar to granny squares (groups of stitches are created in chain spaces rather than in stitch tops), but are an example of another popular type of motif—the circle-to-square. Rounds 1 and 2 create a circle with eight sections. Rounds 3 and 4 use placement of the increases and height of stitches to create four corners and our straight sides—a square! The single crochets of Round 5 provide a stable edge to use in joining squares together.

MATERIALS

YARN

- 1 ball each of 3 colors of light worsted weight yarn
- Size G (4.25 mm) or hook to obtain gauge

NOTIONS

- Large-eyed yarn needle
- One stitch marker

FINISHED SIZE

- Teen/Adult
- Finished circumference (unstretched) at edge = 21" (53.5 cm)
- Height from edge to crown = 9" (23 cm)

GAUGE

- Diameter of completed small flower (Rnds 1–3) = 2½" (6.5 cm). Width of completed motif measured edge to edge = 5 to 5¼" (12.5 to 13.5 cm). Correct gauge is important for finished fit of hat.

STITCHES AND ABBREVIATIONS USED

- chain = ch
- slip stitch = sl st
- single crochet = sc
- double crochet = dc
- stitch(es) = st(s)
- space(s) = sp(s) usually designated by number of chain used to create (i.e. ch-2 sp = space made by 2 ch).
- round = rnd
- place marker = pm

SKILLS

- How to make an entire project by following symbol diagrams, with written directions as supplementary reference

- How to make a circle-to-square motif, useful for additional projects, such as blankets, scarves, and so on

- How to construct a hat from 5 flat squares

- How to wet block a wool or wool blend project

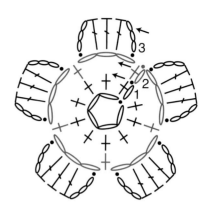

Two colors of ink make the rounds easily visible, but the flower is worked in one color of yarn, without fastening off until completed.

Rnd 2: Ch 1, sc in same st as join, *ch 3, skip next sc, sc in next sc; repeat from * around, joining last ch-3 to first sc with a sl st. {5 ch-3 sps}

Rnd 3: *Sl st in next ch-3 sp, ch 3, 3 dc in same sp, ch 3, sl st in same sp.

Repeat from * in each ch-3 sp around. Fasten off. {5 petals, each consisting of sl st, ch 3, 3 dc, ch 3, sl st}

INSTRUCTIONS

Notes:

1. Stitch counts appear in {brackets} following instructions for rounds.

2. Remember when attaching new yarn colors, to leave sufficient tails for weaving in. It is acceptable to crochet over a starting or finishing tail, but this is only the first stage of the weaving in, and the tail must be long enough to thread onto needle for secure finishing.

3. In this pattern, since chains are worked AROUND and not INTO, it's best to chain rather tightly.

1 **Make Two Small Flowers.** Make one with B and one with C, leaving 10" (25.5 cm) tails at start and finish, for sewing flower to hat. Follow the stitch diagram and refer to the written instructions if necessary.

Ch 5 and sl st to join in ring {5-ch ring}

Rnd 1: Ch 1, work 10 sc in ring, sl st to join last st to first st.

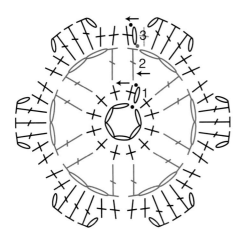

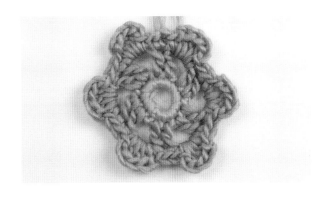

Foundation ring and Rnd 1 are shown in first color; Rnds 2 and 3 are shown in second color. Note the // symbol where first yarn is fastened off.

2 Make One Large, Two-Color Flower. Leave 10" (25.5 cm) beginning and ending yarn tails, for sewing flower to hat.

With C, ch 6, sl st to join in ring. {6-ch ring}

Rnd 1: Ch 1, work 12 sc in ring, sl st to join last st to first st. Fasten off C. {12 sc in ring}

Rnd 2: Attach A with a dc in any stitch, dc in next st, ch 2, *dc in each of next 2 sts, ch 2; repeat from * around, sl st to join last ch to first dc. {6 ch-2 sps, 12 dc}

Rnd 3: Ch 1, * sc in each of next 2 dc, (sc, ch 1, 3 dc, ch 1, sc) in next ch-2 sp; repeat from * around, joining final sc to first sc. Fasten off, leaving long tail for sewing flower to hat. {6 petals}

3 Make Five Circle-to-Square Motifs. With A, ch 5, sl st to join in ring.

Rnd 1: Ch 6, PM in 3rd ch made (counts as dc and ch-3), *dc in ring, ch 3; repeat from * 6 more times, join last ch to marked ch with a sl st. Fasten off A. {8 ch-3 sps, 8 dc}

(continued)

If the Rnd 1 join is done in the turning chain, instead of the top of the first stitch, it will seem like 13 stitches in Round 1 when Round 2 is worked. Be careful to always join the last stitch to the top of the first stitch, to keep the correct number of stitches in each round. Correctly finished Rnd 2 consists of 12 dc and 6 ch-2 spaces.

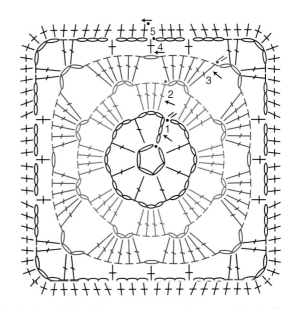

Ink colors in the diagram correspond to yarn colors A, B, and C. Note // symbol when yarn is to be fastened off.

To work between stitches, ignore the Vs at the top, and insert the hook from front to back, between the vertical posts of the two indicated stitches.

Rnd 2: Attach B with a dc in any ch-3 sp, work 3 more dc in same sp, ch 3, *in next sp work 4 dc, ch 3; repeat from * around, ending with a sl st in first dc to join. Fasten off B. {Eight 4-dc groups, 8 ch-3 sps}

TIP *"Any Stitch" Yarn Attachments— Although it's common for symbol diagrams to show the starts of all rounds aligned with each other, when the written directions state that a join may be made in "any stitch," it will actually be easier to do the weaving in of tails if the rounds begin at different places, rather than the straight alignment shown in the diagram. Attach the new yarn in any indicated stitch, and then follow the diagram from the beginning of that round, even though your round is oriented differently.*

Rnd 3: (Note: This round is where the circle begins to change into a square, through varying the length of chain between dc groups. The four evenly spaced longer chains will become the corners of the square, in Rnd 4.) Attach C with a dc in any ch-3 sp, work 5 more dc in same sp, ch 1, *6 dc in next sp, ch 3, in 6 dc in next sp, ch 1; repeat from * 2 more times, 6 dc in last sp, ch 3 (for corner), sl st to join last ch to first dc of round. Fasten off C. {Eight 6-dc groups, 4 ch-1sps, 4 ch-3 sps}

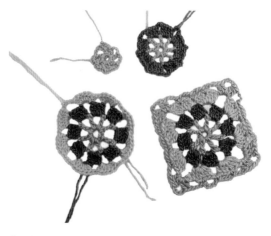

Don't be concerned by the "ruffly" appearance of completed Rounds 2 and 3. The "excess" chain increases will be taken up in Round 4!

Rnd 4: (Note: In Rnd 4 the "squaring process" is completed, through use of taller and shorter stitches, and corner increases.) Attach A with a sc in any ch-1 sp, ch 3, sc BETWEEN 3rd and 4th sts of next 6-dc group (see photo).

Ch 3, (2 dc, ch 3, 2 dc) in corner ch-3 sp, ch 3, sc between 3rd and 4th sts of next 6-dc group, ch 3, *sc in next ch-1 sp, ch 3, sc between 3rd and 4th sts of next 6-dc group, ch 3, (2 dc, ch 3, 2 dc) in corner ch-3 sp, ch 3, sc between 3rd and 4th sts of next 6-dc group, ch 3; repeat from * 2 more times, sl st to join last ch to first sc. Do Not Fasten Off. {20 ch-3 sps, 4 corners worked in taller sts}.

Rnd 5: Ch 1, 3 sc in each of next 2 ch-3 sps, at corner sc in each of next 2 dc, 5 sc in ch-3 sp, sc in each of next 2 dc, *3 sc in each of next 4 ch-3 sps, sc in each of next 2 dc, 5 sc in ch-3 sp, sc in each of next 2 dc; repeat from * 2 more times, sl st to join last sc to first sc. Fasten off. Weave in all yarn tails securely as each motif is completed.

TIP *Why Such a Small Hook/Tight Gauge?—Because a smaller hook, in relation to the size of yarn, creates a stiffer, more structured fabric. These motifs are very open and lacy in their pattern. In order for the hat to hold its shape, the motifs need to be slightly stiff; hence the tight gauge and smaller hook.*

4 **Assemble Hat.** Beginning at the center sc of a 5-sc corner, hold center motif with one side motif, wrong sides together. Matching sts of one side, sc through both thicknesses across. {22 sc}. Fasten off. Repeat with center motif and each side motif, until pieces are assembled as in layout photo below. Next, crochet 4 side seams in same manner, one at a time, from crown to outside edge. {22 sc per seam}. Fasten off and weave in ends, on inside of hat.

5 **Finish Hat with Edging and Flowers.**

EDGING

Rnd 1: With right side of hat facing, attach A with a sc at center of edge of any square. (This is now the back of the hat), sc in each st and in each seam end, around, join with a sl st. Fasten off.

Rnd 2: With right side of hat facing, attach C with a sc in first sc of Rnd 1, sc in each st around, join with a sl st. Fasten off.

Rnd 3: With B, repeat Rnd 2.

Rnd 4: With A, repeat Rnd 2.

Weave in all yarn tails, on inside of hat.

Make sure that the right side of each motif is facing up in the layout. This will make it easy to be certain to crochet them together correctly.

SEW FLOWERS TO HAT

Position flowers on hat, as desired. Sew into place, using flower's yarn tails. Weave in any remaining yarn tails.

BLOCKING

If your yarn is wool or wool blend, wet blocking will help the wool soften, and will relax the stitches into a natural relationship with one another, creating a "finished" look to the fabric and the project.

Begin by soaking the hat in cool water with a little of one of the following: delicate washing product such as Woolite, white vinegar, or a non-rinse product such as Soak or Eucalan. Allow the hat to soak submerged in cool water for 15 to 30 minutes. Pour off the water, and squeeze excess water out of the hat, being careful NOT to twist or wring. If using a product requiring rinse, soak for 5 minutes or so in clear water and squeeze the clear water through the hat before pouring off. Roll the hat in a dry towel and squeeze the roll to remove most of the water. Gently lay the hat out on another dry towel, and shape it so that there are no areas with curling or crookedness. Allow hat to dry, out of direct sun. When dry, the hat is ready to wear, and should be soft and smooth.

pattern stitches

Most crochet fabrics are not actually comprised of rows or rounds of a single stitch. The open lace and infinite textures that characterize crochet are created by use of pattern stitches.

A pattern stitch is any regularly repeating sequence comprising combinations of basic stitches. Some pattern stitches are fairly simple and the sequence develops within a single row. Others are quite complex, with a repeated pattern both within each row, and one that develops over the course of several rows.

In this chapter, some other common single-row stitch patterns will be explored, and the project, Cozy Cowl and Cuffs, will put several pattern stitches to work. In addition, this chapter introduces the use of lighter weight yarn, looser gauge appropriate for soft, lacy fabrics, and techniques for the management of color pooling.

practice swatches

Single Crochet Pattern Stitches

SINGLE CROCHET RIBBING STITCH

We'll start with the simplest pattern stitch, single crochet ribbing. This pattern actually only uses one stitch—single crochet—but the stitches are worked, row by row, in the back loop only, creating a corrugated effect. The resulting fabric is much more stretchy than regular "flat" single crocheted fabric. Often, the cuffs of sweater sleeves, the edging of a neckline, or the band area of a hat will benefit from a bit of stretch, and this simple pattern stitch is one way to provide that. When used in one of these ways, the sc ribbing is generally worked in relatively short rows, and then the whole piece turned on its side, so that the rows run vertically, in the direction that the cuff should stretch and bounce back. However, whole scarves, blankets, or sweaters can also be made from ribbed fabric.

MATERIALS

YARN
- 3 yarn scraps, 20 to 25 yds (18.5 to 23 m) each, worsted weight

HOOK
- H or I (5 or 5.5 mm)
- Yarn needle
- 2 stitch markers

SKILLS

- How to make 3 different pattern stitches that use combinations of single crochet and chain stitches

- How to determine the multiple and decide on the correct number of chains to start with for each pattern stitch

- How to measure gauge in a pattern stitch

Here's the stitch symbol diagram for single crochet ribbing:

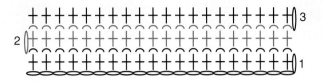

And here are the written directions:

Ch 21. Note: all stitches are worked in back loop only (blo).

Row 1: Sc in blo of 2nd ch from hook, and each ch across, ch 1. Turn. {20 sts}

Row 2: Sc in each st across, ch 1. Turn.

Repeat Row 2 to desired length.

Work a swatch of 20 stitches, for 6–8 rows, till the pattern of working in back loops only seems comfortable and familiar.

TIP *Use "negative ease" to make ribbings snug. If a sleeve cuff needs to go snugly around a 9" (23 cm) wrist, the unstretched piece, as crocheted, might only need to be 7½" (19 cm) in length, depending on the inherent stretch in the yarn.*

Both strips consist of 15 rows of 7 stitches each. Top: unstretched, as crocheted; bottom: stretched.

GRANITE STITCH

A pattern stitch may go by different names in different generations or parts of the world. This stitch is also sometimes called "stepping stones." However, symbol diagrams help to determine whether two names refer to the same pattern stitch or not. This pattern consists of (sc, ch1) with successive rows worked in the ch-1 spaces.

Here's the symbol diagram for Granite Stitch:

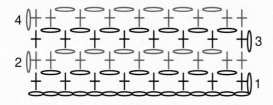

And here are the written directions:

Ch 16 (an odd number, plus one for turning)

Row 1: Sc in 2nd ch from hook, *ch 1, skip 1 ch, sc in next ch; repeat from * across, ch 1. Turn. {8 sc, 7 ch-1 spaces}

Row 2: Sc in first st and in next ch-1 sp, *ch 1, skip next sc, sc in next ch-1 sp; repeat from * across to last sc, sc in last sc, ch 1. Turn. {9 sc, 6 ch-1 spaces}

Row 3: Sc in first st, *ch 1, sk next sc, sc in next ch-1 sp; repeat from * across to last 2 sc, ch 1, sk next sc, sc in last sc, ch 1. Turn. {8 sc, 7 ch-1 spaces}

Repeat Rows 2 and 3 for pattern, to desired length.

PETITE SHELLS, OR MINI SHELLS OR SINGLE CROCHET V STITCHES

This is another pattern stitch with many names. It's a great one, by any name, for creating a solid but stretchy and soft fabric. In regular rows of single crochet, the stitches and strands of yarn comprising them, all relate to one another in perpendicular angles, reducing stretch and creating structure instead of softness. Taller stitches have more softening diagonals in them, but leave relatively large holes in the fabric between stitches. This pattern angles the single crochets on diagonals, providing soft drape and stretch, while still producing a solid fabric.

Here's the stitch symbol diagram:

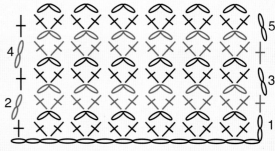

Granite stitch. The top three rows have been worked in alternating colors, to emphasize the pattern created by working in chain spaces instead of tops of stitches.

And here are the written directions:

Ch 16 (any even number, plus 4)

Row 1: (Sc, ch 2, sc) in 4th ch from hook (petite shell made), * skip next ch, work petite shell in next ch; repeat from * across to last 2 ch. skip next ch, sc in last ch. Turn. {6 petite shells}

Row 2: Ch 2, *petite shell in each ch-2 sp across, ending with sc in ch-2 sp formed by turning chain of previous row. Turn.

Repeat Row 2 for pattern, to desired length.

Petite shells. In the top row, petite shells have been worked in alternating colors, to emphasize placement of shells in ch-2 spaces at center of shells in previous row.

STITCH MULTIPLES

When stitches are used in repeating patterns, the number of stitches in the starting chain is controlled by the "stitch multiple." This term refers to the number of stitches it takes to complete one of the repeating sequences. For instance, in the diagram for the Petite Shells, it's fairly easy to see that each shell takes the space of 2 chain, and then the sequence begins the next repeat. So, the stitch multiple for Petite Shells is 2. This means that any even number will work—a smaller number for a shorter row, a larger even number for a longer row. But, in addition to the actual multiple of the pattern stitch, there are also usually one or more chains for turning (two in the example). There may also be one or more stitches at either end of the row that allow for stability in the fabric, straight edges as the rows progress, and also set up the base for the following row of the pattern. These stitches must be added, not to each repeat, but to the total for the row. In our example swatch, the row of seven shells at a stitch multiple of 2, means we need 14 ch, and we also need one for the last stitch of the row and two for the turn. In directions this would be expressed as "Chain an even number plus 3."

practice swatches

Double Crochet Pattern Stitches

The next few pattern stitches are created mainly with double crochet stitches and use a larger number of beginning chain. A stitch will always state the number of the multiple plus the extra chain needed for the first row's beginning, ending and turning. The directions for the next few stitch patterns also contain this important information.

V-STITCH

The V-stitch, usually abbreviated V-st, consists of a double crochet, one or more chain, and another double crochet, all worked into the same stitch or space. V-st makes a very soft, pliable fabric with medium-sized holes. It has a lacy appearance, a good amount of stretch and drape because of the diagonals, and is warm but still breathable.

Here's the stitch symbol diagram:

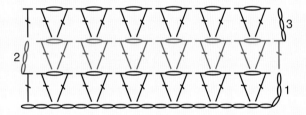

And here are the written directions:

Chain a multiple of 3, plus 4. The practice swatch shown below has a starting chain of 22 (18 + 4).

Row 1: (Dc, ch 1, dc) in 5th ch from hook (V-st made), *skip next 2 ch, V-st in next ch; repeat from * to last 2 ch, skip 1 ch, dc in last ch. Turn. {22 ch start = 6 V-sts}

Row 2: Ch 3 (counts as first dc). V-st in each ch-1 across, ending with dc in top of turning chain. Turn.

Repeat Row 2 for pattern, to desired length.

MATERIALS

YARN

- approximately 20 yds (18.4 m) each of worsted weight yarn scraps

HOOK

- H or I (5 or 5.5 mm)

SKILLS

- How to read the diagrams and directions for three pattern stitches based on the double crochet stitch, and make swatches of each ○ How to measure gauge in a multi-stitch pattern repeat

- How to read the diagram and written directions for a pattern stitch that uses both single and double crochet stitches, and make a swatch

V-stitch. Row 4 has been worked in a contrasting color, to emphasize the placement of the individual V-stitches.

THE WONDERFUL WORLD OF SHELLS

There are innumerable pattern stitches based on the idea of working several dc in the same space, so the tops of the stitches fan out to cover as much space as a straight row, but in a softer, stretchier, more decorative pattern. Most shells contain an odd number of stitches, so that the following row's stitches can be centered, with identical numbers of stitches before and after the center of the shell. However, if more 2 or more stitches are going to be worked in the center of the shell, a ch-1 space is often substituted for the dc at the shell's center. This is because of that familiar offset between the stem and top of a dc stitch. When the top of the stitch is stretched out large by having 5 or so stitches worked into it, the offset is more visible, and the shell appears lopsided, with more than half the stitches pushed to one side and fewer than half on the other side of center. The problem is solved by using a ch in the midst of the shell, as will be seen in the first pattern stitch below, which is a simple Stacked Shells pattern. The Cozy Cowl and Cuffs Set on page 103 uses another stacked shell variation, but MANY other variations of Stacked Shells also exist, and there are whole stitch dictionaries devoted to the nearly infinite variety of shells.

STACKED SHELLS

Here's the stitch symbol diagram for the pattern stitch:

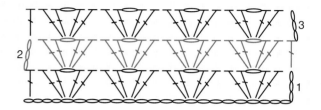

Here are the written directions:

Worked over a multiple of 5 stitches plus 6.

Shell: (2 dc, ch 1, 2 dc) all worked in indicated stitch or space.

Ch 26 (20+6).

Row 1: Work shell in 7th ch from hook, *skip next 4 ch, shell in next ch; repeat from * across to last 4 ch, skip next 3 ch, dc in last ch. Turn. {4 shells}

Row 2: Ch 3 (counts as first dc), shell in ch-1 sp at center of each shell across, ending with dc in top of turning ch 3. Turn. {4 shells}

Repeat Row 2 for pattern, to desired length.

Stacked shells. Rows have been worked in alternating colors to emphasize placement of each shell in the central space of a shell in the previous row.

STAGGERED SHELLS

Staggered shells is a pattern that produces a softly textured fabric without large holes. Because each row of shells sits between the shells of the previous row, alternating rows must begin and end differently, requiring two rows to repeat for the pattern. Each row does have the same number of shells, but in even-numbered rows, one shell is split, with a "half-shell" at each end. Because the following row makes only one sc in the center of each shell, the shells do not have a ch-1 space at their centers.

Here's the symbol diagram:

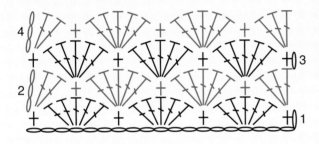

And here are the written directions:

Worked over a multiple of 6, plus 1 (with 1 additional ch needed for foundation).

Shell = 5 dc all worked in indicated stitch.

Ch 20 (18+1+1).

Row 1: Sc in 2nd ch from hook, *skip next 2 ch, shell in next ch, skip next 2 ch, sc in next ch; repeat from * across. Turn. {3 shells}

Row 2: Ch 3, 2 dc in first st (half-shell made), sc in 3rd (center) dc of next shell, *shell in next sc, sc in center dc of next shell; repeat from * across, ending with 3 dc in last sc (2nd half-shell made). Turn. {2 shells, 2 half-shells}

Staggered shells. The half-shells beginning and ending Rows 4 and 6 have been worked in contrasting color, to make it easy to see them. Note that the half-shells provide a straight smooth edge to the fabric.

Row 3: Ch 1, sc in first st, shell in next sc, *sc in center (third) dc of next shell, shell in next sc; repeat from * across, ending with sc in top of turning ch. Turn. {3 shells}

Repeat rows 2 and 3 alternately for pattern, to desired length.

In many project patterns using pattern stitches, the pattern sequence groups, such as V-st or Shell will be defined at the start of the pattern, in the section with stitches and abbreviations. It's important to read this section, because the pattern sequences will be counted like a single stitch in the rest of the instructions, and the directions will only tell you to "make a shell" or "work a V-st," etc., rather than instructing each component of the sequence. It's also important to measure gauge carefully in projects requiring fit. Often the gauge will be stated as "so many shells and so many rows = so many inches (centimeters)," or "so many pattern repeats = so many inches (centimeters)." Measure as normally, being sure to place the beginning of the measurement at the beginning of a repeat, and count the repeats as if they were single stitches.

CRUNCH STITCH

The final pattern stitch for this chapter is made by alternating sc and dc stitches in a row. When measuring gauge, each pair of stitches counts as a repeat. In alternating rows, the tall stitches are worked on top of short ones, and vice versa. The fabric formed has a soft, nubbly texture, and because the posts of the dc stitches are bent between shorter adjacent stitches, there's a lot of stretch inherent in the fabric. It's a great one for socks, sweaters, baby blankets—any project that needs a fabric without holes and with stretch.

Here's the diagram for Crunch Stitch:

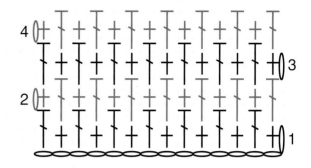

And the written directions:

Worked over an even number of stitches, plus 1.

Ch 15 (14+1).

Row 1: Sc in 2nd ch from hook, dc in next ch, *sc in next ch, dc in next ch; repeat from * across. Turn. {7 pairs of sc/dc}

Row 2: Ch 1, sc in first st, dc in next st, *sc in next st, dc in next st; repeat from * across. Turn. {7 pairs of sc/dc}

Repeat Row 2 for pattern, to desired length.

Gauge: two shells = 2½" (6.5 cm)

Crunch stitch. The top (6th) row has been worked in alternating colors to emphasize stitch placement.

COZY COWL AND CUFFS SET

The relationship between the diameter of the hook and the size of the yarn is an important factor in determining the drape and softness of fabric.

For this project you will use a large hook H or J (5 or 6 mm) with sock weight yarn, to create a softly draping, wearable lace. At first, handling the finer yarn may feel awkward. It may be necessary to adjust the way yarn is held for tension and flow. Experiment a little as you work swatches for gauge—but don't measure the stitches till you've worked several rows of stitches at an even, comfortable tension. It's probably easiest to start with the largest hook and the loosest pattern stitch, which are used for making the cowl. Then "graduate" to smaller hooks for the cuffs.

MATERIALS

YARN
- 450 yds of sock/fingering weight yarn

HOOKS
- F or G (3.75 or 4.25 mm)
- H and J (5 and 6 mm)

NOTIONS
- Large-eyed needle
- Stitch markers (1 necessary, up to 5 optional)

FINISHED SIZE
- Cowl is one size, 14½" wide, 30" circumference (37 × 17 cm)
- Wrist warmers in two sizes: S/M fits wrist up to 6½" (16.5 cm) measured 1" (2.5 cm) above wrist bone. M/L fits wrist up to 9½" (24 cm) measured 1" (2.5 cm) above wrist bone

GAUGE
- With F hook, in sc ribbing, 21 sts and 25 rows = 4" (10 cm)
- With G hook, in sc ribbing, 19 sts and 23 rows = 4" (10 cm)
- With H hook, in Stacked Shell pattern, 3 pattern repeats = 4" (10 cm), 5 rows = 3" (7.5 cm)
- With J hook, in V-stitch pattern, 6 V-sts = 4½" (11.5 cm), 5 rows = 3" (7.5 cm)
- Gauge is not essential for cowl, but is necessary for fit of cuffs. Adjust hook size as necessary to maintain correct gauge

(continued)

MATERIALS

STITCHES AND ABBREVIATIONS USED

- chain = ch
- slip stitch = sl st
- single crochet = sc
- back loop only = blo
- double crochet = dc
- stitch(es) = st(s)
- space(s) = sp(s)
- round = rnd
- place marker = pm
- move marker = mm
- V–stitch = V–st; in indicated st or sp, work (dc, ch 1, dc)
- shell = sh; in indicated st or sp, work (2 dc, ch 2, 2 dc) see diagram for stacked shell pattern below

SKILLS

- How to manage tension to create soft fabric with thinner yarn and a large hook
- How to use pattern stitches in the context of a project pattern, to create a soft cowl and wrist warmers set

COZY COWL

Notes:

1. Stitch counts appear in {brackets} at end of individual row or round instructions.

2. Use of a blended yarn with 10%-25% (or more) nylon will add stretch to the cuffs. It is NOT recommended to use a non-stretching yarn, such as 100% cotton.

1 **Make Main Section of Cowl.** With J (6.00mm) hook, and leaving a 10" tail for sewing, ch 124.

TIP *Use stitch markers, every 20 or 25 ch, to help keep accurate count.*

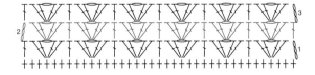

Row 1: Dc in 5th ch from hook (counts as ch 1, dc), ch 1, dc in same ch (first V-st made), *skip 2 ch, V-st in next ch; repeat from * across to last 2 ch, sk 1 ch, dc in last ch. Being careful not to twist work, sl st last dc made to top of first dc, to join. Use tail to sew first and last stitch together from join just made, to beginning ch edge. Work now proceeds in joined rounds. {40 V-sts, 1 dc at each end of row}

Rnd 2: Ch 3, PM in 3rd ch made , V-st in ch-1 sp of each V-st around, ending with a sl st to join final st to marked ch. MM to top of beginning ch of each rnd as work progresses.

Rnds 3-21: Repeat Rnd 2.

2 Bottom Granite Stitch Edging.

Rnd 22: Ch 1, sc in each dc and in each ch-1 sp around, ending with sc in beginning ch-1. Work now proceeds in spiral. {121 sc}

Rnd 23: Ch 1, skip 1 st, sc in next st, PM in ch-1 sp just made to mark beginning of rnd. Continue to MM to first ch-1 sp in each round, *ch 1, skip next st, sc in next st; repeat from * around.

Rnd 24–26: Continue to work rnds in Granite Stitch pattern (sc in next ch-1 sp, ch 1, skip next sc). At end of Rnd 26, sl st to join last st to marked ch-1 sp. Fasten off, remove marker.

3 Top Granite Stitch Edging and Finishing.

Rnd 1: With right side of cowl facing (for right side, select the side that looks the best to you), attach yarn to opposite side of beginning chain, starting at seam joining ends of Row 1. Repeat Rnd 22 of bottom edging, working into loops at the bases of the dc sts.

Rnds 2–5: Repeat Rnds 23–26 of bottom edging. At end of Rnd 26, fasten off and weave all yarn tails in securely.

TIP *To weave in the ends securely in this open pattern, run the needle up through the center of a dc stitch, then up through the center of the stitch in the next row. This is the first direction— remember it takes 3 directions of stitching to make a secure finish. Next, run the needle under the base of a V-st, and then through the centers of the chains between V-sts. In this way, pass through 3 or so V-sts. This is the second direction. Finally, run the needle down through the centers of several rows of dc stitches. Tug the last stitch run gently, and cut carefully close to the fabric.*

COZY CUFFS

Make 2.

Directions for both sizes are the same, but use an F hook at stated gauge for the smaller size. Use G hook at stated gauge for larger size.

1 **Make the Ribbed Wrist Section.** With F or G (3.75 or 4.25mm) hook (or hook needed to obtain correct gauge for desired size), leave a 14-16" tail for sewing, and ch 25.

Row 1: Sc in 2nd ch from hook and each ch across. Turn. {24 sc}

Row 2: Ch 1, sc in blo of each st across. Turn.

Rows 3–36: Repeat Row 2. At end of Row 36: Ch 1, rotate work 90 degrees, to work in ends of rows.

2 Make Hand Section.

Row 1: Work 1 sc in each row end across, ending with 2 sc in final row end. {37 sc}

Row 2: Change to H (5.00mm) hook, ch 3 (counts as first dc), *skip 2 sts, shell (see Stitches Used) in next st, skip 2 sts, dc in next st; repeat from * across. Turn. {6 shells, 7 dc}

Row 3: Ch 3, *shell in ch-2 sp of next shell, dc in next dc; repeat from * across. Turn.

Rows 4–6: Repeat Row 3. At end of Row 6, ch 3, join with an sc in top of beginning ch 3.

3 **Edging of Hand Section.**

Rnd 1: Sc in each st and each ch-1 sp of Row 6, sc in each of 3 ch, sl st in joining sc. Fasten off.

FINISHING

Using tail left at start, matching stitches, whip stitch together Row 36 and opposite side of beginning chain of ribbed section.

multi-row stitch patterns—lovely lace!

In this chapter, we'll explore stitch patterns that develop over several rows. Multi-row pattern stitches require careful row counting! Pattern stitches can be developed over any repeating number of rows, most commonly between two and seven rows per repeat. The practice swatches and project presented in this chapter require three rows per repeat. This means that the directions and symbol chart will detail the foundation and "set up" rows (in which the pattern is established) and then direct that certain rows are repeated in order, over and over.

This chapter also introduces a new stitch: the treble(or triple) crochet, abbreviated as tr in patterns. This stitch is one loop taller than a double crochet. When added to the arsenal of basic stitches, it provides a wider variety of options in stitch and row height, and adds much to the open, "holey" appearance of many lace patterns. When the treble stitch and following a repeating row sequence are mastered, you'll be ready to make the lovely triangular lace shawl on page 000. Let's start with the new stitch.

Standard stitch symbol for treble crochet (tr). Note 2 hash marks on the stem, as opposed to the dc symbol, which has 1 hash mark. Hash marks in stitch symbols denote the number of times to yarn over at the beginning of the stitch.

A NEW STITCH—TREBLE (OR TRIPLE) CROCHET

The treble crochet (tr) stitch is very similar to the double crochet (dc), except that it starts with an extra yarn over, and is completed with an extra "yo and pull through 2 loops," doing that step 3 times instead of the 2 times for dc. The standard turning chain to start a row of trebles is 4 chain. So, to learn the stitch, start with a row of 10 sc (ch 11, sc in 2nd ch from hook and each ch across). Just as in a row of dc, the first stitch is skipped, as the turning chain stands in place of that stitch. If necessary, the first stitch and last stitch of each row can be marked with stitch markers, as a reminder.

1 Yarn over twice and insert the hook into the second stitch of the row. Yarn over and draw a loop through the work. There are now four loops on the hook.

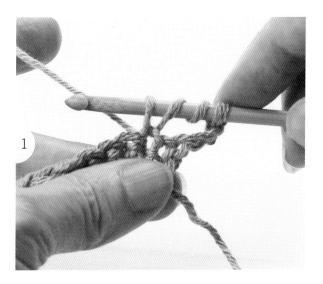

(continued)

Completed first row of treble stitches, with turning chain to start second row.

3 Repeat steps 1 and 2, working in each stitch across the row, until there are 10 trebles, including the turning ch-4 at the start of the row. Chain 4 to start the next row, marking the 4th chain (top of the turning chain) if necessary, as a reminder to count it as a stitch and work a stitch in that spot in the following row.

4 Work several more rows, until the stitch is familiar and comfortable.

2 Yarn over and pull through two loops. Now there are three loops on the hook (A).

Repeat the (yo and pull through 2) two more times, reducing the number of loops on the hook by one, each time (B). After the third repeat, there will be one loop on the hook again, and the first treble stitch is complete (C).

Working into the top of the turning chain, to complete Row 2

practice swatch

Multi-Row Pattern Repeat

Having mastered the basic stitches, the two most important factors to keep in mind now, are remembering to start each row with the correct number of turning chain, and whether to work in or to skip the first stitch of the row. The number of turning chain will always be stated in a well-written pattern. The number of chain may differ, depending on the first stitch of the row, and whether the turning chain is to be counted as a single stitch, or as a tall stitch and length of additional chain. Our practice swatch will be worked in solid rows, each consisting of only one stitch type, so the only issue is to remember to work in the first stitch if making single crochet and to skip the first stitch and work in the turning chain at the end, if the stitches are double or treble crochets. Treble stitches in any row are counted in the same manner as double crochets: either count the sideways Vs at the tops of the stitches, or count the vertical posts. The post has two diagonal twists on its right side, and three small bumpy knots on its reverse or "wrong" side. In the swatch, the fabric is reversible, with each kind of stitch appearing as both right side and wrong side rows in the progression.

1 **Foundation:** Ch 16.

Row 1: Sc in 2nd ch from hook and in each ch across. Turn. {15 sts}

2 **Row 2:** Ch 3, dc in each st across. Turn. {15 sts}

Row 3: Ch 4, tr in each st across. Turn. {15 sts}

Row 4: Ch 1, sc in each st across. Turn. {15 sts}

MATERIALS

YARN
- 20 yds (18.4 m) or so of scrap yarn, worsted weight

HOOK
- Size G7 (4.5 mm) or H (5 mm), whichever is most comfortable

NOTIONS
- 2 stitch markers for top of turning chain and last stitch in row(optional)

SKILLS

- How to appropriately vary turning chain length for different stitches
- How to keep track of rows in a multi-row pattern repeat
- Confidence and familiarity with switching between familiar and new stitches

Repeat Rows 2–4 for pattern. Make your swatch at least 4 full repeats (13 rows). To keep track of the row being worked, it helps to use a small sticky note. Position this marker on the pattern directions indicating the current row, and then move it at the start of each row. The number of completed repeats can be penciled onto the paper marker.

(continued)

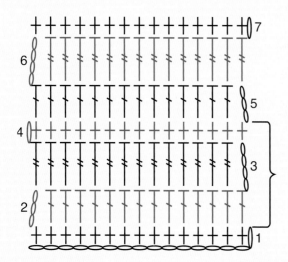

Stitch Symbol Diagram: *Work from the diagram, the written directions that follow, or both, depending on personal preference. Note that the diagram's placement of turning chains is a reminder of whether or not to count the turning chain as the first stitch of each row.*

Completed swatch with arrows marking sc rows to make counting repeats easier.

TROUBLESHOOTING

If after several rows, there are more or fewer stitches per row than the ten you started with, check to make sure the first stitch of each row is skipped, and that a stitch is worked in the top of the turning chain at the end of each row. See page 61.

The most common difficulty particular to the treble stitch, is that often the last loop worked off the hook, which forms the top of the stitch, ends up much larger than the others, as seen here:

It's not that the whole stitch is too loose, but just the top, and it can be very frustrating! The answer lies in managing the loops on the hook, while the stitch is being worked. The problem results from there being too much space between the loops on the hook, which includes extra yarn in the stitch:

Note that the loops are widely spread on the hook, leading to extra space in the top of the stitch.

Hold the loops closely together while working them.

Another cause of "big top syndrome" is tension irregularity as the stitch is worked. If the left hand does not allow enough yarn to flow into the stitch at each (yo and pull through 2) stage, all the tension of the stitch is at its base, and the top gets very loose. Conversely, if each loop is pulled through with a generous amount of yarn, it results in a small and appropriate top loop.

Left hand properly allows the hook to pull a generous amount of yarn through each time the (yo and pull through 2) phase is worked.

It may seem counterintuitive, but the more yarn allowed into the stitch as loops are pulled through, the tighter the top of the stitch becomes!

Work at least ten rows of trebles, paying attention to tension and to keeping the loops gathered together on the hook.

WINDFLOWER SHAWLETTE

Whether worn to warm shoulders on a breezy evening, or to welcome the change of seasons as a softly draping scarf, the Windflower Shawlette provides opportunity to use many of the stitches learned so far, and to practice a multi-row pattern stitch. This little shawl (or large scarf) shows what can be done with fine weight yarn, a large hook, and a pattern that repeats over three rows. For luster and drape, choose a yarn with fine texture, blending another natural fiber with some silk, rayon, or bamboo. And don't worry if the project looks bunchy and lumpy while in process; the magic of blocking will "open up" the lace, as long as natural fibers make up most of the fiber content.

MATERIALS

YARN

- 435 yds (400.2 m) fingering weight or lace weight merino/silk blend

HOOK

- J (6 mm)

NOTIONS

- Large-eyed yarn needle
- One stitch marker

GAUGE

- Gauge is not important for this project, but it's important to use a relatively large and loose gauge, in order to get proper drape and softness in the finished fabric. Gauge in the sample, before blocking, in sc rows: 15 sts = 4" (10 cm), Rows 1–9 of pattern = 4" (10 cm) in height

STITCHES AND ABBREVIATIONS USED

- chain = ch
- single crochet = sc
- double crochet = dc
- treble crochet = tr
- shell = sh: work 5 tr in indicated stitch
- stitch(es) = st(s)
- space(s) = sp(s)
- round = rnd

SKILLS

- How to make a triangular lace shawl of any size, starting at the bottom tip
- How to follow a multi-stitch, multi-row lace pattern, in both written and diagram formats
- How to block a lace project by the "soak and pin out" method of wet blocking

INSTRUCTIONS

Notes:

1. Stitch counts follow row directions, in {brackets}.

2. Ch 4 at the beginning of any row counts as first treble st of the row.

3. Optional: Use a stitch marker in the 4th ch of ch-4 row beginnings, to mark top of turning chain.

4. Optional: Use a sticky note to keep track of diagram or written pattern rows as they are worked.

5. Finished size is flexible, and the shawlette can be made in any size, as desired. Sample is made with 1 skein of yarn. To make a full-sized shawl, work extra rows until desired size is reached. To make a kerchief or headscarf, work fewer rows, and follow the bonus instructions for edging ties.

TRIANGLE, STARTING AT BOTTOM POINT.

Foundation: Ch 5, 4 tr in first ch made. {5 tr (shell)}

Row 1: Ch 1, sc in each st across. Turn. {5 sc}

Row 2: Ch 1, sc in first sc, *ch 3, skip 1 st, sc in next st; repeat from * one more time. Turn. {3 sc, 2 ch-3 arches}

Row 3: Ch 4, 4 tr in first st (first shell made), *dc in next sc, sh in next sc; repeat from * across. Turn. {2 shells, 1 dc}

Row 4: Ch 1, sc in each st across, including top of ch-4 turning ch. Turn. {11 sc}

Row 5: Ch 1, sc in first sc, (ch 3, sk 1 st, sc in next st) twice, sc in each of next 2 sts, (ch 3, sk 1 st, sc in next st) twice. Turn. {4 ch-3 arches, 7 sc}

Row 6: Repeat Row 3, working one additional shell. {3 shells, 2 dc}

Row 7: Repeat Row 4. {17 sc}

Row 8: Ch 1, sc in first sc, (ch 3, sk 1 st, sc in next st) twice, *sc in each of next 2 sts, (ch 3, sk 1 st, sc in next st) twice; repeat from * across. Turn. {6 ch-3 arches, 11 sc}

Repeat Rows 6, 7, and 8, working one additional shell each time the sequence is repeated. Shell counts are as follows:

Row 9 = 4 shells

Row 12 = 5 shells

Row 15 = 6 shells, etc.

Row 30 = 11 shells

Row 45 = 16 shells

Row 57 =20 shells

Sample was worked to a width of 20 shells, leaving enough yarn on one skein of Charlemont to work the edging. At end of Row 57, or at desired size, do not fasten off.

SHAWLETTE EDGING.

Rnd 1: Turn the work and repeat Row 4 one more time, working a row of sc across the top of the triangle. Rotate the work when the side edge is reached. Now work down the row ends, working around, rather than into the stitches.

Ch 1, work 1 more sc in the same stitch, and then space 100 loosely crocheted sc evenly down the side of the triangle to the point of the triangle, if the triangle is exactly 57 rows. If the triangle is more or fewer pattern repeats, be sure to work this round so that the number of stitches down the side of the triangle is a multiple of 8, plus 4 ($8 \times 12 = 96$, $+ 4 = 100$).

In the point of the triangle, the base of the foundation shell (the first shell worked in foundation step above) work 3 sc. Mark the center sc of these 3. Evenly space 100 stitches (or the correct multiple of $8 + 4$ for the number of rows), up the final side of the triangle.

This first edging round sets up the base for the decorative border, so take time to make sure the stitch count has the correct multiple. When each diagonal side of the triangle has 100 sc and there are 3 sc at the point, turn.

Rnd 2: Ch 1, sc in first st, *ch 5, sk 3 sts, sc in next st*; repeat from * to * 24 more times, ch 7, skip marked "tip" stitch, sc in next st, repeat from * to * 24 times, ch 2, dc in final sc, making last arch finish with hook at top center of arch. Turn. {25 ch-5 arches on each side, 1 ch-7 arch at tip}

Rnd 3: Ch 1, sc in same arch, *(3 dc, ch 3, 3 dc) in next arch, sc in next arch; repeat from * 11 more times, in ch-7 arch at tip, work (5 dc, ch 3, 5 dc), sc in next arch, **(3 dc, ch 3, 3 dc) in next arch, sc in next arch; repeat from ** across. Fasten off.

TIP *When any pattern directs that a certain number of stitches be "evenly spaced" along an edge, there is a simple method for working the correct number of stitches. Fold the edge in half and mark the center stitch. Fold each half in half and mark the stitches at each fold. Now the edge is divided into fourths. Longer edges may require more divisions; shorter edges require fewer. Next, if the edge is divided into fourths, simply work ¼ the total number of stitches before reaching the first marker, ½ before the second marker, etc. In the current example, there will be 25 stitches between each set of markers. The marked "tip" stitch is not part of that count. Working the correct number of stitches in the first marked section is the hardest, but once accomplished, it gives a "feel" or sense for how closely together the stitches need to be worked.*

FINISHING

Weave in all ends securely. Block by soaking in a wool-soak product or water/vinegar solution.

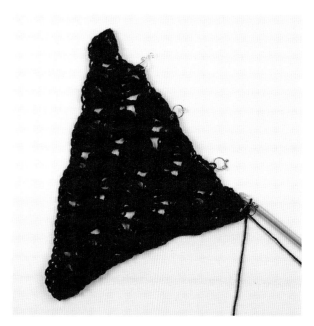

In this small-scale sample, first side of triangle edge has been worked, tip stitch marked, and second side marked off in fourths for even spacing.

WET BLOCKING

Lace always benefits from being "opened" by first thoroughly wetting the fibers and then stretching out the stitches, allowing the fabric to dry under tension. In the steps that follow, a smaller sample is used to show wet blocking.

1 Place the completed shawlette in a large bowl or tub, and fill with cool water and the manufacturer's recommended amount of nonrinse wool soak. Alternatively, 1 tablespoon of white vinegar added to 3 or 4 quarts of water will accomplish the same thing, but with vinegar fragrance. (rinsing before proceeding to the next step will remove vinegar scent—simply repeat this step with clear water.) Allow the shawlette to soak for at least 20 minutes, but up to overnight is fine. It takes time for every fiber to fully absorb water.

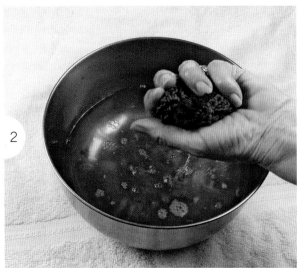

2 Carefully lift the item from the water, squeezing out as much water as possible, but absolutely avoiding stretching, wringing or pulling on the fabric. Ball it up and squeeze! Lay the wadded item on a clean towel and discard the water.

3 Remove more water by rolling the item in a towel. Lay flat on the length of the towel and roll just like a wet swimsuit. Squeeze the roll by hugging it, to move as much excess water as possible from the item to the towel.

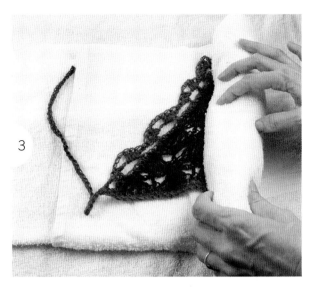

4 For the next step, any surface will suffice as long as it's clean, can be pricked by pins and will remain undisturbed for 24 hours or so. Foam "Blocking Boards" and "Blocking Mats" are available commercially, but many people use a towel-covered spare bed mattress, or the foam floor mat sections sold for children to play on. Lay out the item, flat, on the chosen surface. Starting at the center, gently smooth and stretch outward to the edges. When the item is flat and spread, start at one corner or tip (bottom tip of the shawlette in this case). Place a pin to hold the center of the ch-3 space at the shawlette's tip.

Continue working up the sides, alternating from one side to the other, spreading, stretching, and placing a pin to hold tension on each ch-3 space. These will become "points" in the edge of the lace, and greatly add to its beauty and "finished" appearance. Don't worry if several pins need to be re-positioned during the process. As long as the fiber is still damp, the pins are moveable. When satisfied with the even stretch of the item, leave it alone till thoroughly dry.

5 Remove pins; clip any yarn ends that appear, close to the surface of the fabric. The shawlette is now complete!

a new stitch

Having learned the chain, slip stitch, single crochet, double crochet, and treble, there is just one more basic stitch to know—the half-double crochet (hdc). Half-doubles create a thicker, more cushiony fabric than the other crochet stitches.

THE HALF-DOUBLE CROCHET
Making the Hdc

Here's the diagram symbol for the hdc. It's similar to the symbol for the dc, but there is no diagonal slash on the stem.

Start with a chain of 16.

Row 1: Yarn over, insert hook in 3rd ch from hook, and draw up a loop. So far this is just like starting a double crochet stitch. There are 3 loops on the hook.

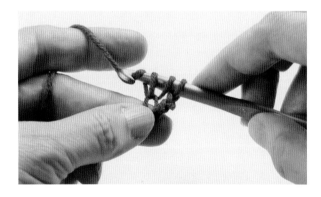

Yarn over and pull through all three loops. (1 hdc made)

Work across the row, making one hdc in each chain. Turn the work and ch 2.

At end of the first row, there are 14 hdc stitches and a turning chain.

Now there is a decision to be made, and it's purely a personal one. In single crochet, the turning chain is always 1 and does not count as a stitch—the first sc of the next row is made in the stitch immediately below the turning chain. In working double crochet, the turning chain is 3, and counts as a stitch—the first actual stitch being made in the second available stitch of the row. The half-double crochet has no such rule. The correct height for the turning chain is 2, because the new row of stitches is 2 loops tall. But whether that turning chain counts as the first stitch of the row or not is the "gray area." If it is counted as a stitch, that turning chain is noticeably thinner than all the other stitches in the row. On the other hand, if the ch-2 is not counted as a stitch, the edges of the work will have a wavy appearance, rather than straight lines, because of the ch-2 loops at the ends of the rows. Usually, in patterns using hdc, the designer specifies at the start, which option has been chosen. While it does affect the numbers for stitches in the row in the pattern, it's by no means a law that must be followed.

Many crocheters actually have come up with other solutions. Some people turn, ch 1, sc in the first st, ch 1 (for added height) and then proceed with the row of hdc, starting with the second stitch. This creates an actual stitch at the row end . . . but it doesn't look exactly like the others in the row. Another method preferred by many, is to turn, slip stitch in the first stitch and then chain 2, counting that as a stitch. It's still a bit thin, but stands squarely over the last stitch of the last row, and doesn't leave a hole. Other crocheters choose to ch 1 at the turn, pull up the loop slightly so the ch-1 is a bit taller than usual, and then work the first hdc in the first stitch. As you work your swatch, experiment with the different turning options, and choose the one that looks best to you with the yarn and hook you're using. The main thing is to be consistent throughout any given project and to remember whether the turning chain is being "counted" or not . . . being careful, therefore, of the stitch counts for the row being worked in the pattern. The swatch below shows each of the turning chain options used for three rows.

There are some textural distinctives of the hdc fabric. It has a definite horizontal ridge that shows in every other row on either side of the fabric when worked back and forth in rows. When worked in the round, the ridges are all on the wrong side of the fabric, and the front is quite smooth. That ridge provides extra possibilities for locations of insertion; many "fancy" stitches are actually variations on hook insertion in a hdc row. For the slippers project on page 121, regular, top of- the-stitch placement is used.

Bottom three rows: ch 2 not counted as a stitch, side edge loops evident.
Rows 4–6: Ch 2 counted, holes appear because end stitch is thinner than others.
Rows 7–9: (Sl st, ch 2) counted as a stitch, no holes, but the end stitch is still "thin."
Rows 10–12: Ch 1, draw loop up a little not counted as a stitch, first hdc made in first stitch, no holes, straight edge to fabric, uniform stitches all the way across.
Rows 13–15: (Ch 1, sc, ch 1) counted as a stitch.

ANY FOOT SOFTY SLIPPERS

These simple slippers are so versatile! Make them in infant size as a baby shower gift; make them in child sizes as holiday gifts; and larger sizes for the men in your life. Optional leather soles can be purchased online or at craft and yarn shops, and add durability to the comfort. They can be made in school or college colors—solid, striped, or color blocks! Only the size of your gift list limits the variety of slippers to be made!

MATERIALS

YARN

- 35 to 70 yds (32.3 to 64.4 m) of sport or worsted yarn for infant or small child sizes
- 75 to 100 yds (69 to 92 m) of worsted yarn for larger child or small women's sizes
- 150 to 200 yds (138 to 184 m) for most women's sizes
- 200 to 300 yds (184 to 276 m) for larger mens' sizes
- To work with doubled yarn, for added thickness, double the amount of yarn and increase hook size

HOOK

- Size F or G (3.75 or 4.25 mm) hook for sport weight yarn (Infant sample slippers worked with G [4.25 mm] hook)
- H or I (5 or 6 mm) hook for worsted weight yarn (I [5.5 mm] hook used for child and adult sample slippers)
- J (6 mm) hook used for holding worsted yarn doubled, as in man's sample

NOTIONS

- Large-eyed yarn needle
- Optional leather sole in appropriate length
- OR optional "puffy" fabric paint for non-skid soles
- Measuring tape
- Pencil and plain or quad-ruled/graph paper

SKILLS

- How to use measurements and a schematic drawing to custom fit a project
- How to choose the "right" hook and gauge for a project when not stated
- How to make comfy slippers for any size foot

PLANNING THE PROJECT

For this project, there are three measurements to take. Those measurements will be applied to the schematic drawing, and then gauge will be used to determine the number of stitches needed to achieve those measurements. In this way, ANY foot measured can be fit for the slippers, and you'll gain an understanding of the way patterns are designed.

◢ **TIP** *If making infant bootie/slippers as a shower gift, there is no little foot to measure! Newborn size booties or slippers usually have a 3" to 3½" (7.5 to 9 cm) sole length, and it works quite well to use the same measurement for #1 and split the length in half for #3. This formula was used to make the sample infant-sized slippers.*

1 Measuring the Foot.

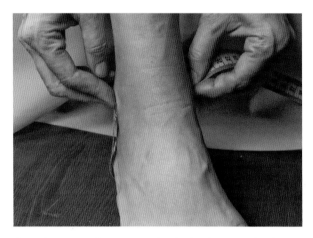

Pass the measuring tape under the heel, measuring from one ankle bone to the other, and note the measurement as "#1."

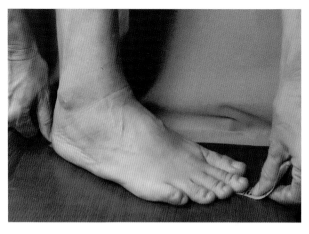

Measurement #2 is from the heel to longest toe.

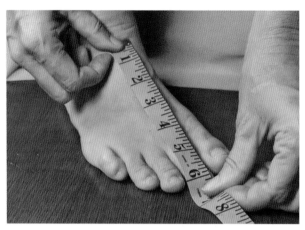

The final measurement is the length of the top of the foot, from ankle crease to toe. Subtract this number from #2 and note the answer as #3 on the drawing. This gives the distance for the opening at the top of the slipper.

2 Finding Gauge for the Project and Calculate the Length of the Foundation Chain. With the yarn you've chosen, work three different 10 stitch by 10 row swatches, each using a different hook. The three hooks should be the one suggested above for the yarn type, one slightly larger and one slightly smaller. Feel the swatches, and look at them closely. Which one appeals most as a thick, soft, solid fabric?

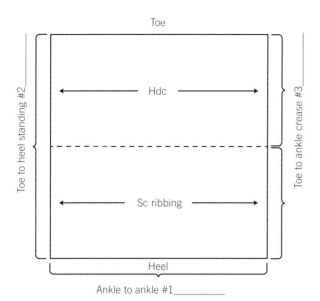

Toe

Toe to heel standing #2

Hdc

Sc ribbing

Toe to ankle crease #3

Heel

Ankle to ankle #1_____

Schematic drawing with measurements labeled. Use graph paper or plain paper to make a drawing for your project. The lines don't need to be straight, and it doesn't need to be "to scale." Write the measurements taken so far in the appropriate places on the drawing.

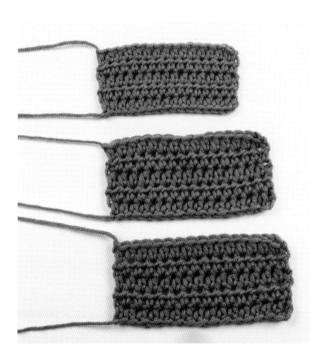

These swatches each have the same number of stitches and rows, all in hdc with ch 1 (drawn up tall) turns; they were made with the same yarn by the same crocheter. The size difference is entirely due to hook. Top to bottom: G (4.25 mm) hook, H (5 mm) hook, I (5.5 mm) hook.

Having chosen a hook, measure the stitches achieved with it. Count the number of stitches in one inch (2.5 cm) of a row. If there are 4 stitches in an inch (2.5 cm), and measurement #1 was 8" (20.5 cm), then it will take (4 × 8 =) 36 stitches to cover that distance. Of course the foundation chain will also need to include a turning chain. We'll be starting with some rows of sc in blo, so add 1 (the turning chain) to the total and you're ready to start the project! If there is a fraction in the stitches per inch, and/or a fraction in measurement #1 (4½ stitches per inch [2.5 cm] and 6½" [16.5 cm] for #1, for example) the multiplication problem here results in an answer with a fraction in it = 29¼. Simply "round it up" to the next higher whole number and work 30 stitches per row. Half a stitch can't be crocheted, after all!

③ Crochet the Rectangle with Tie Loops.

Foundation: Leaving a 12" to 15" (30.5 to 38 cm) tail, start with the chain calculated in Step 2.

Row 1: Sc in 2nd ch from hook and each ch across. Turn.

Row 2: Ch 5 (for tie loop . . . how it works will become apparent when slipper is assembled), sc in blo in each stitch across. Turn.

Repeat Row 2 until piece is as long as #3 on the schematic drawing. Turn, but do not fasten off unless changing colors. If changing colors, fasten off here and attach the new color as the next row begins.

When the piece's length equals or is just barely over the "#3" length on your schematic, begin to work in rows of hdc, worked through both top loops of the stitch, using your choice of turning method at the end of each row. There is no need, in this part of the slipper, for the extra long chains at turning— we're past the ankle opening of the slipper.

(continued)

3

When the whole piece measures equal to or just over the #2 length (total length of foot), fasten off, leaving at least a 36" (91.5 cm) tail.

tell me more

A **FLOAT** is a length of yarn not worked into any stitch, but being carried along the work until needed again. Floats often occur at the ends of rows in striped work, and can run along the back of other work with color changes within a row.

TIP *If stripes are desired for the heel section, simply work 2 rows of each color, alternating. Change colors in the last stitch of the second row of each color, and carry the other color on the same side of the work each time…this will become the inside of the slipper and the float will not be apparent once the tie strings are threaded through the loops and the slipper is right side out.*

Assemble the Slipper. Thread the long ending tail onto a large-eyed yarn needle and run a stitch along the ends of the row just completed, catching just one loop from the top of each hdc stitch. Pull firmly on the tail, and the end of the rectangle will curl up in a tightly gathered circle. Pull tightly enough that there is no visible hole in the center of the circle just created. Now make a small locking stitch by inserting the needle under the first and last stitch (the ends of the row, where they now meet each other). Repeat 2 or 3 times, for sturdiness (A).

With the same yarn still threaded on the needle, make sure that the slipper is facing wrong side out. This won't be evident if only one color has been used, but if stripes were worked, the side with the yarn floats is the wrong side of the work—the inside of the slipper. Make a whip-stitch seam, joining the ends of the hdc rows. When the seam reaches the transition to sc ribbing rows, again work a locking stitch, as above, and fasten off.

(B) Next, thread the yarn needle onto the beginning tail, fold the foundation chain at the heel end of the slipper in half, and sew a whipstitch seam. Weave in all ends.

4A

4B

6

5 **Ties (make 1 for each slipper).** Chain three times the number of stitches used for the foundation of the slipper in step 2. Sl st in each ch across. Fasten off and weave in both yarn ends. This is the same method as used for ties in Chapter 4. Use the crochet hook to pull the tie through the ch-5 loops at the ends of the ribbing rows, so that the center of the tie is centered at the heel seam and the ends are at each side of the seam at the top of the foot.

TIP *Ties can be made in the same color, one of the stripe colors, or any color as whimsy dictates! Once threaded, a knot tied right at each end of the tie makes it easier to use, and helps prevent the tie coming out of the loops in the laundry.*

6 **Non-Skid Slipper Soles (optional).** Ready made leather slipper soles are available online, or in yarn shops or craft stores. Purchase the size closest to the actual foot measurement taken in step 1. When the slipper is assembled, use the pre-drilled holes in the leather to whipstitch the sole to the slipper, being careful to center the heal seam and top of foot seam in line with the end points of the sole. Slippers with leather soles are NOT machine washable! Follow the manufacturer's cleaning instructions for any leather item.

Infinite variety is possible when using this method of project planning! Measure, draw a schematic, find gauge, and voila—you're designing your own projects!

abbreviations

Here is the list of standard abbreviations used for crochet.

approx.	approximately		**oz**	ounce(s)
beg	begin/beginning		**p**	picot
bet	between		**patt**	pattern
BL	back loop(s)		**pc**	popcorn
bo	bobble		**pm**	place marker
BP	back post		**prev**	previous
BPdc	back post double crochet		**qutr**	quadruple triple crochet
BPsc	back post single crochet		**rem**	remain/remaining
BPtr	back post triple crochet		**rep**	repeat(s)
CC	contrasting color		**rev sc**	reverse single crochet
ch	chain		**rnd(s)**	round(s)
ch-	refers to chain or space previously made, e.g., ch-1 space		**RS**	right side(s)
ch lp	chain loop		**sc**	single crochet
ch-sp	chain space		**sc2tog**	single crochet 2 stitches together
CL	cluster(s)		**sk**	skip
cm	centimeter(s)		**Sl st**	slip stitch
cont	continue		**sp(s)**	space(s)
dc	double crochet		**st(s)**	stitch(es)
dc2tog	double crochet 2 stitches together		**tbl**	through back loop(s)
dec	decrease/decreases/decreasing		**tch**	turning chain
dtr	double treble		**tfl**	through front loop(s)
FL	front loop(s)		**tog**	together
foll	follow/follows/following		**tr**	triple crochet
FP	front post		**trtr**	triple treble crochet
FPdc	front post double crochet		**tr2tog**	triple crochet 2 together
FPsc	front post single crochet		**WS**	wrong side(s)
FPtr	front post triple crochet		**yd**	yard(s)
g	gram(s)		**yo**	yarn over
hdc	half double crochet		**yoh**	yarn over hook
inc	increase/increases/increasing		**[ ]**	Work instructions within brackets as many times as directed.
lp(s)	loop(s)		*****	Repeat instructions following the single asterisk as directed.
Lsc	long single crochet		*** ***	Repeat instructions between asterisks as many times as directed or repeat from a given set of instructions.
m	meter(s)			
MC	main color			
mm	millimeter(s)			

TERM CONVERSIONS

Crochet techniques are the same universally, and everyone uses the same terms. However, US patterns and UK patterns are different because the terms denote different stitches. Here is a conversion chart to explain the differences.

US	UK
single crochet (sc)	double crochet (dc)
half double crochet (hdc)	half treble (htr)
double crochet (dc)	treble (tr)
triple crochet (tr)	double treble (dtr)

about the author

Deb Burger learned to crochet from her grandmother at age 12. While she has found enjoyment in many artforms, crochet remains her lifelong favorite. She has been teaching crochet for the past 20 years through Girl Scouting, various community centers, summer camps, at Charlotte's Fibers (a yarn shop in Western North Carolina), and the John C. Campbell Folk School. She is active in the online community, Ravelry as Cerdeb, and has written articles and patterns for Interweave Crochet and the e-zines Crochet Insider and Crochet Uncut.

index

fibers
  gauges, 14, 40, 122
  holding, 21
  language of, 18
  self-striping, 51
  thread, 13
  winding by hand, 17
  yarn, 14–16, 51

hooks
  gauges, 11, 19
  holding, 20–21
  inline hooks, 11, 19
  materials, 11, 12
  parts of, 10
  shapes, 10–11
  sizes, 10, 11, 12, 14, 40
  tapered hooks, 11, 19
  tips, 10

language
  asterisks, 42, 56
  back of the work, 22
  bloom, 18
  bouclé, 18
  chain stitch, 24
  cupped circles, 49
  decreasing, 58
  float, 124
  front loop only, 53
  front of the work, 22
  gauges, 40
  graphic symbols, 84
  halo, 18
  hank, 16
  loft, 18
  parentheses, 56
  pattern language, 31, 36, 56
  ply, 18

right side, 22

ruffling, 49

skein, 16

slubs, 18

stitch multiples, 97

tail, 22

thick, 18

thin, 18

turning chain, 36

twist, 18

working yarn, 22

wrong side, 22

yarn over, 24

notions, 19

practice swatches

  chain stitches, 25

  charts, reading, 85, 86, 87

  crochet in the round, 44–48, 86

  crunch stitches, 101

  double crochet stitches, 60–62, 63, 64, 98–101

  granite stitches, 96

  granny squares in one color, 70–72

  granny squares in three colors, 74, 87

  multi-row pattern repeat, 109–110

  pattern language, 37

  petite shells, 96–97

  shells, 96–97, 99–101

  single crochet, 37, 94–97

  stacked shells, 99

  staggered shells, 100

  V-stitches, 98

projects

  Any Foot Softy Slippers, 121–125

  Bright and Bold Coasters, 39–43

  Chain Gang Boa, 27–31

  Cozy Cowl and Cuffs Set, 103–106

  Flower Power Retro Beanie, 89–93

  Grab-and-Go Granny Bag, 77–81

  Longitude Scarf, 67–69

  Phone Carrier, 55–59

  Roll Brim Cloche, 51–53

  Windflower Shawlette, 113–117

techniques

  back loop only, 55–59

  chain stitches, 23–24, 27–31

  charts, reading, 84–87, 89–93, 98–101

  circle-to-square motifs, 91–93

  crochet in the round, 44–48, 51–53, 55–59

  custom fittings, 122–123

  double crochet stitch, 60–65, 67–69

  edging, 33, 37, 41–42, 72, 74, 79, 80, 93, 105, 106, 115

  front loop only, 51–53

  gauge measurements, 40, 95–97, 122–123

  granny squares, 70–75, 77–81

  half-double crochet, 118–119, 121–125

  motif connections, 77–81

  multi-row stitch patterns, 107–110, 113–117

  pattern language, 36, 37, 39–43

  pattern stitches, 94–101, 103–106

  single crochet stitches, 32–36, 39–43

  slip knots, 22, 27–31

  solid stitch motifs, 77–81

  steam blocking, 43

  stitch combinations, 94–97, 109–110

  stripes, 51–53, 67–69, 124

  tension management, 104–106

  treble (triple) crochet, 107–108

  wet blocking, 93, 116–117

  working in spiral, 44

troubleshooting

  chain stitches, 25

  crochet in the round, 49, 52

  curling, 37

  double crochet stitch, 65

  gauge measurements, 40

  granny squares, 73, 75

  multi-row pattern repeat, 111

  single crochet stitches, 35, 37